CYH

66-17927 (R-7-69)

NEHRU: THE YEARS OF POWER

NEHRU

THE YEARS OF POWER

GEOFFREY TYSON

FREDERICK A. PRAEGER, *Publishers*
New York · Washington · London

FREDERICK A. PRAEGER, *Publishers*
111 Fourth Avenue, New York 10003, N.Y., U.S.A.
77-79 Charlotte Street, London W.1, England

Published in the United States of America in 1966
by Frederick A. Praeger, Inc., Publishers

© 1966, Geoffrey Tyson, London, England

Library of Congress Catalog Card Number: 66-17927

PRINTED IN GREAT BRITAIN

TO KATHLEEN
who shared with me so many
happy Indian years

CONTENTS

FOREWORD

MORE THAN ONCE in the recent past I imagined I had written the last word of this book, but then something occurred to make it seem that I ought to add a few stop-press pages to deal with such matters as the Rann of Kutch, the Indo-Pakistan conflict or some other event that might reasonably be assumed to flow from Pandit Nehru's policies. And I have, in fact, done so. But the very real necessity to set a *terminus ad quem* to any piece of writing has precluded all but the briefest reference to the Tashkent conference and its sad sequel in the death of L. B. Shastri, or to Indira Gandhi's subsequent elevation to the high office which her father occupied with such distinction for seventeen years.

I am, of course, indebted to many friends—both British and Indian—for the interchange of ideas which have contributed to such merits as this book may possess. They are too numerous to mention by name. For the opinions expressed and its inevitable defects, I alone am responsible.

London, February 1966   GEOFFREY TYSON

NEHRU: THE YEARS OF POWER

I

THE MAN AND THE NATION

WHEN JAWAHARLAL NEHRU DIED on the morning of May 27, 1964, he joined the company of the immortals; for he had given a nation shape and a new purpose in life. For more than a quarter of a century he had devoted himself to the cause of his country's independence, and he spoke movingly on that day in August 1947 when, at last, he took the oath of office: 'Long years ago we made a tryst with destiny. Now the time comes when we redeem our pledge. . . . ' He was then fifty-eight years of age, and for the next seventeen years until he was seventy-five and death claimed him, he continued to be prime minister of India.

This book is not a biography, definitive or otherwise. It is an attempt to assess the years of power, the years in office which we now realise were all too short for the achievement of the many things he had planned for India. But it is nonetheless desirable to mark the chief events in the life of a man who led the world's second most populous nation to freedom, who lived in the age of Churchill and was a septuagenarian in the company of Macmillan, Khrushchev, Eisenhower, de Gaulle and Tito, with all of whom he bestrode the stage at a moment of profound change.

Jawaharlal Nehru was born in 1889 at Allahabad, son of a prosperous and distinguished Kashmiri brahmin lawyer, Motilal Nehru. His family had migrated from Kashmir via Delhi two hundred years earlier at the invitation of the Moghul Emperor Farrukhsiar. Motilal Nehru was a liberal and an

admirer of western culture. He sent Jawaharlal, his only son, to
England to be educated at Harrow and Trinity College,
Cambridge, where he took his degree in Natural Science. On
leaving Cambridge he read Law and was called to the English
bar, and on his return practised without any great distinction at
the Allahabad High Court.

About the time of the first world war he began to take an
active part in political life. He joined the All-India Congress
and was elected to its Committee in 1918. He found it rather
tame and thought the Congress programme of those days too
passive. As a sideline he began to take an interest in the Kisan
(peasant) movement in Oudh, and it was here that he first
gained a reputation as a speaker able to sway large outdoor
audiences. It was on these occasions also that he first felt the
radical and revolutionary urge which was to dominate his later
years in the struggle for freedom. Meanwhile he had come under
the spell of Mahatma Gandhi and the two men, so unlike in
many ways, formed a partnership behind which millions of
Indians rallied. The Satyagraha movement, with its programme
of civil disobedience, was launched in 1919. Inevitably it
brought Nehru into conflict with the authorities, in consequence
of which he served the first of what were to be nine prison
sentences under British rule.

Gradually he became an increasingly important figure in the
Congress Party, and between 1923 and 1939 held first the
office of secretary and then of president, the latter no less than
three times. He studied not only Indian but world affairs and
travelled several times to Europe, where he maintained his
friendship with leading intellectuals—particularly the leaders
of the British Labour Party. In 1939 he went to China. When
the second world war broke out, Nehru said to that lifelong
friend of India, Edward Thompson, 'everyone knows that your
cause is right'. But he maintained that the war was not India's
war, since the country had not attained full independence.
That remained his attitude throughout. It brought him to
prison once more in 1940, and again at the beginning of the
'August Movement' in 1942, when he was sent to the fort at
Ahmednagar where he wrote *The Discovery of India*—a survey of
Indian civilisation through the ages. He thus joined Sir Walter
Raleigh, John Bunyan and the ranks of other famous prisoners

who have made great contributions to literature during the
period of their detention.

After the war he was released and took part in the negotiations with Lord Wavell and the British cabinet mission. No
settlement was found which would satisfy all parties, but an
interim Indian government was set up with Nehru as minister
for Foreign Affairs and Commonwealth Relations, and vice-
president of the viceroy's Executive Council. He had also once
again become president of the Congress Party. Finally, during
Lord Mountbatten's term of office as viceroy there came the
agreement which set up the two independent sovereign states
of India and Pakistan. It is impossible to measure precisely the
contribution which the close friendship that developed between
Pandit Nehru and Lord Mountbatten made to this final
settlement between Britain and India; but it was considerable.
With the premiership of the state of India, Nehru combined the
office of minister for External Affairs, and from time to time he
held other portfolios, including that of Atomic Energy. In later
years he was to be criticised for attempting to do too much.

On subsequent pages we shall deal in more detail with some
of his many-sided activities. Mention, however, may here be
made of one. During his first years of office he was much
occupied with the problem of India's becoming a republic,
which he had long regarded as its proper status. At the 1949
Conference of Commonwealth Prime Ministers, there was
evolved the London Declaration, ratified by the Indian
parliament the following month, whereby India remained
within the Commonwealth when it became a republic in
January 1950. Thus, on Pandit Nehru's initiative, was provided a formula for future entrants to the Commonwealth in
which he believed strongly and which, as an institution, he was
at all times prepared to defend with fervour and eloquence.
While he saw in group treaty organisations something that
would almost certainly hamper India's freedom of action,
membership of the Commonwealth seemed to him to carry no
such restrictive provisions. He lived to become the doyen of
all Commonweath premiers and the longest serving member of
their periodical conferences.

Nehru was continuously in office for seventeen years. He fought three general elections on the basis of universal franchise and a genuinely secret ballot, and on each occasion brought his party home to victory. This is something quite unique in Asia which, by and large, is not enamoured of the ballot-box as an instrument of government. In foreign affairs he discarded the purely negative side of neutralism and non-alignment (i.e. he interpreted it as something more than non-intervention) and gave these concepts a practical meaning, while at home he showed that economic planning, as expressed in the Five Year Plans, can be made to work inside a democracy which is still in the first stages of gestation. There were, of course, many failures as well and they will be noted on later pages. But the achievements are such as to merit mention here and now.

India is widely regarded as perhaps the most important member of the 'uncommitted' world. This may well be true, but what would seem to be of more importance is that it has set a working pattern for nearly all those smaller developing countries which have followed India along the road to freedom during the last decade and a half. In part this has been because India has provided an example of a parliamentary democracy in action, served by a well trained civil service and a competent and impartial judiciary. The country has also benefited from the possession of an alert, mature and sophisticated business class. But its influence abroad—particularly in Asia and Africa —was very largely of Pandit Nehru's own personal making. In him the whole underdeveloped world, and especially that part of it which lies within the Commonwealth, felt it had a spokesman who commanded wide attention. It is true that Communist China has now begun to compete strongly for the goodwill of the African and South Asian groups of states; but until recently India managed to hold its position within the Afro-Asian group, though since the debacle which overtook its forces in the Himalayas, it is no longer regarded as its leader and exemplar. It is the purpose of this book to try to define what it is that Nehru did in his seventeen years of office which raised him to the special position he enjoyed both inside and outside his own country, as well as to see what he has left undone.

It is frequently remarked that very little of Gandhism remains in India today; it will be our business to try to calculate how much of Nehruism (assuming there is such a thing) is likely to survive his departure from the scene in which he played a dominating role. Nehru's critics allege that one of his conspicuous defects was that for too long he kept every possible rival or successor at arms length, that no one was allowed to understudy him. The charge will be discussed on a later page; all that need be said now is that, if it was true, the allegation is one commonly made against politicians everywhere, and there are no grounds for thinking that Indian politicians are greatly different from the rest. There is also some evidence that not a few responsible Indians were relieved that Nehru's successor was not so much of a globe trotter, moved by a recurring urge to put the world to rights.

Whereas African nationalism is a creation of the last twenty or thirty years, Indian nationalism goes back very much further than most men now living can recall. The Indian National Congress Party held its first meeting in Bombay in 1885. In any estimate of Nehru's career account must be taken of the fact that with 'Rajaji' (C. Rajagopalachari, now in his eighty-fifth year) Nehru was the last surviving member of Gandhi's old guard who fought the independence struggle from the days immediately following the first world war. Lacking the Socratic qualities of Rajaji, he nevertheless possessed a unique magic with which he could both sway the multitude and, at a different level of advocacy, influence the small decision-making inner circle of Congress leaders. At the same time, while often appearing to be withdrawn and alone, Pandit Nehru in his prime was alert to the slightest change of the political temper. This intuitive quality seems to have partly deserted him during his last years. With his final illness and the passing of the years he became slower to respond to the moods of his people, and competent observers who were close to him consider that Goa (December 1961), followed by the general election of early 1962, marked the climax of an inner conflict in a man who, probably more than most statesmen, often gave the impression that he was at close grips with some great moral or political issue. It will be recalled that the Indian prime minister suffered a by no means trivial illness in the spring of 1962, by which time the strain of office had clearly become well nigh insupportable. Afterwards the humiliating China episode, other anxieties

and the mild stroke of January 1964 took further heavy toll of
Nehru's ebbing strength and authority.

Politicians are popularly supposed to have some special or
secret source of inspiration. It is not easy for an outsider,
particularly a westerner (even though he may have long
personal experience of India itself), to say precisely what influence buoyed Nehru up through these long and anxious years.
Unlike Mahatma Gandhi, he was no mystic. But no one who
saw him in contact with the enormous crowds which are the
inevitable accompaniment of political activity in India can
have the slightest doubt that at least some part of his inspiration came from the masses, to whom he always talked with an
easy fluency and understanding. In this respect he did resemble Mahatma Gandhi, who possessed the same powers of
communication—perhaps communion would be the better
word—with the people. Thus, notwithstanding the rather
complicated party and parliamentary machine, Nehru was
always able to appeal to the electorate directly, and in this
sense he operated one of the purest forms of democracy. But,
of course, the difficult business of governing a great nation of
over 400 million cannot be carried on by the simple process of
a dialogue between national leader and people.

Pandit Nehru took over the government of India as a going
concern whose administration, though temporarily under strain,
was of the highest quality. In this respect he was fortunate, for
it is doubtful whether he would have been able to enlarge the
functions of government in the way that he did if he had not had
at his disposal an experienced and versatile civil service, ready
to adapt itself to a whole range of new tasks. To take only two
examples: the entire machinery of planning had to be created
and independent India's role in foreign affairs recognised by
the proper staffing of a diplomatic service of some quality.
(India has today 129 representational missions overseas.) The
integration into India of the former princely states and the
orientation of policy in the direction of an Asian welfare state
were other main planks in the Nehru policy which made
further heavy demands on a civil service of high calibre but
limited numbers. We shall consider these matters later on, but
the point now is that Nehru had to work with limited resources

as much of manpower as of finance: a condition which is not always to the liking of someone who by nature plans on the grand scale and is impatient to get on with the job. He did not spare himself in the service of his country and he expected his officers to show something of the same devotion to duty. In many matters Nehru often presented a picture of a man in a hurry seeking to make up the leeway of centuries in a decade or two. Joan Robinson says that perhaps the outstanding problem of the present day is 'the relatively slow economic development of India under institutions imitated from parliamentary democracy contrasted with that of China under the direction of the Communist Party. Western Liberalism has only warmed the surface of the deep waters of Indian tradition. . . .'[1] Nehru was, in fact, a typical product of nineteenth century European liberalism, who knew by instinct the optimum speed at which his country could be driven forward. 'The pragmatic approach' was a phrase he frequently used, and pragmatism as a system of thought admits the existence of doubt and the possibility of error, both of which are excluded from the Marxist dialectic.

Though twenty years is a long span in the life of a man, it is but a moment in the life of a nation. One suspects that in spite of the known limitations, Nehru had almost certainly hoped for more progress in all directions than, in fact, India was able to make. In a moving and oft-quoted speech which he made to the Constituent Assembly on the night of August 14, 1947, he said:

Long years ago we made a tryst with destiny, and now the time comes when we shall redeem our pledge, not wholly or in full measure but very substantially. At the stroke of the midnight hour when the world sleeps India will awake to life and freedom. A moment comes which comes but rarely in history, when we step out from the old to the new, when an age ends and when the soul of a nation, long suppressed, finds utterance. It is fitting that at this solemn moment we take the pledge of dedication to the service of India and her people and to the still larger cause of humanity.

Stepping out from the old to the new was indeed the task of the Nehru administration, and at a brisk pace; but what, in the

practical terms and conditions of their daily life, has the process
meant to the people of India? To govern and order one's own
affairs represents, of course, an immediate accretion of self-
respect which only those who have lived unfree can properly
understand and measure. But freedom, liberty—whatever you
choose to call it—is a general condition; it is what men do with
their liberty that counts. And in India there have always been
so many worthwhile tasks crying out to be done that a ruler
with more idealism than experience might in 1947 have been
pardoned if he hardly knew where to commence. Nonetheless,
a beginning had to be made.

Of the difficulties which faced Nehru at the outset of his
administration, the special problems arising from the division
of the subcontinent were quite the most formidable and, in one
form or another, many of them are still with his successors.
Partition was organised roughly on the basis of religious
differences, according to whether Hindus or Moslems were in
the majority at various points on the map. But where religious
differences are not of a clear-cut kind, pointing to no obvious
predominance of one sect over another, they do not necessarily
provide satisfactory criteria for the definition of boundaries.
Nor do they always take account of economic factors. The mass
movement of refugees, in which it is estimated that over 12
million people crossed the Indo-Pakistan borders in each
direction by mid-1948, with accompanying loss of life and
property that beggars description, represents but one of the
pains of parturition accompanying the birth of independent
India and Pakistan. The Kashmir quarrel has its genesis in the
same unhappy and ever-present dichotomy, which means that
the possibility of an outbreak of communal bloodshed is never
very far below the surface.

If the integration of several hundred princely states had not
been carried out with a skilled and sure hand by the late
Sardar Vallabhai Patel, the subcontinent might easily have
suffered division into a third major segment in which the smaller
princely states would have grouped themselves round the more
powerful rulers in independent blocs, with resultant balkanisa-
tion of a large part of the land. The arrangements made for
terminating the old relationship of the states with the govern-

ment in Delhi, and with the Crown in London (the complicated doctrine of 'paramountcy'), were perhaps the least satisfactory of all those designed to ensure a smooth transfer of power from British to Indian hands. Apart from the religious factor, which Nehru was genuinely anxious to play down, the facts of geography determined whether the princely states would adhere to India or to Pakistan. Many were unprepared for the abrupt plunge they had to take, often from a semi-medieval form of rule, into the politics of the subcontinent; and in effect they were told they enjoyed an option which did not in truth exist.

The drafting of a new constitution was a major undertaking which had to be pushed forward at the same time as other far-reaching events were taking place, and ministers' minds were preoccupied with what can now be seen to have been matters of life and death for thousands of Indians. Two weeks after India became independent, the Indian parliament, sitting as a constituent assembly, set up a drafting committee of seven under the chairmanship of the late Dr B. R. Ambedkar, which produced a first draft of a constitution in the short period of six months. It drew substantially on British experience, and in particular upon the Government of India Act of 1935. Eight months later, the constituent assembly began detailed consideration of the constitution bill, which lasted a year and embraced discussion of approximately 2,500 amendments. A final session was held on January 24, 1950, and two days later Dr Rajendra Prasad was elected the first president of the Indian Republic. Consisting of 395 articles and 9 schedules, the Indian constitution is said to be the longest in the world. It has since been the subject of seventeen amendments, one or two of which are of major importance. It is based on the concept of the secular state which Pandit Nehru regarded as ideal for the government of a country in which religious stresses are most pronounced. Even after the act of partition, 45 million Moslems remained in India.

Pandit Nehru's socialism considerably antedated Indian independence, and to many people it is surprising that the idea of an economic plan for India was not given formal shape until 1951 when the First Five Year Plan was inaugurated. But in the first flush of independence there were many other matters competing for his attention besides economic planning, and it is known that his deputy prime minister, Sardar Vallabhai Patel, who died in 1950, had no great confidence in the modern planner or his works. Thus, despite Nehru's enthusiasm, it was not until 1950 that a planning commission, with himself as chairman, was established 'to formulate a plan for the most effective and balanced utilisation of the country's resources', to 'appraise from time to time progress achieved', and to examine 'the principal problems affecting the social and economic development of the country'.

The First Plan for the five years from April 1951 to March 1956 was a modest affair, and most of its targets were comfortably reached or exceeded. But it gave the administration the necessary self-confidence to embark on more ambitious projects in the Second Plan. The Five Year Plans have caught the imagination of the free world as nothing else has about India. Almost certainly the planning owes its inception and execution to Nehru himself, and in this respect his influence on India's economic growth must last for at least the rest of this century. 'The central objective of public policy and of national endeavour since Independence', say the authors of the Second Five Year Plan Outline, 'has been promotion of rapid and balanced economic development.'

The Second and Third plans have run into various difficulties which have been much publicised and, as might be expected of economic operations on this scale, serious setbacks have been encountered from time to time; but Nehru's basic philosophy of planning within a free society by and large stands justified, and will surely rank as one of his main achievements for India.

In foreign policy the record is much more uneven, and the more noticeable because this is a portfolio which Pandit Nehru always supervised himself. His full title was 'Prime Minister and Minister of External Affairs and also in charge of the Department of Atomic Energy'. In so far as India had a foreign policy at all prior to 1947, it was as an adjunct to British foreign policy in which it played an important but subordinate functional role deriving from India's geographical position and the high quality and (for the times) mobility of the Indian army. The civil and military branches of the Indian establishment were an important—indeed essential—part of the Pax Britannica, but they were only a part acting in concert with other parts. The Foreign and Political Department was responsible for staffing the missions in, and maintaining good relations with, border and neighbouring states such as Nepal and Afghanistan. Indian troops were available for policing local trouble spots in the eastern hemisphere, and the Royal Indian Marine was responsible for similar duties in the Persian Gulf and the adjacent waters of the Indian Ocean. But there was no separate, autonomous, coherent and distinctively Indian foreign policy; India was essentially part of the vast complex of machinery by which the Pax Britannica was maintained.

And yet it would be wrong to say that India before independence had no views or opinions of its own on international affairs. From time to time Congress passed resolutions which were critical of external policies that were being pursued by Britain in India's name, and in 1925 the All-India Congress Committee established a foreign department and appointed Pandit Jawaharlal Nehru as its head. The department had few of the resources necessary for the study of a highly specialised subject. Inevitably, it was largely concerned to protest against India's entanglement in matters which Indians did not then consider as their affair. The present-day policies of 'non-alignment' and 'non-involvement' undoubtedly owe something to the negative thinking of forty or more years ago. So far as foreign affairs were concerned, India began its independence with a clean slate and very little experience of the subject on the part of either the politicians or the civil service.

India's search for a foreign policy is one of the most fascinating aspects of the first twenty years of the new democracy's history. We shall look at it in greater detail later on. Meanwhile, it can be said that, in spite of its apparent naivety and contradictions, non-alignment makes sense to most educated Indians, though since the frontier war with China they have become increasingly sceptical of such lofty philosophical abstractions as *Panch Shila* (the Five Principles of Peace). The inadequacy of policy has perhaps been most obvious in India's dealings with Pakistan. But responsibility for failure is at least as much Pakistan's as it is India's, and there is some evidence that middle-aged men and women in each country, who grew up in an undivided subcontinent, find it difficult to think of the other as being in the field of 'foreign policy'. Non-alignment does not, of course, preclude full support for the United Nations nor, on occasion, a definite alignment with the Afro-Asian group for no better reason than that it is indicting the sins of the colonial past of some European power. On the many occasions on which he has led the Indian delegation in the General Assembly, or appeared before the Security Council, Krishna Menon has not always presented the best possible image of his country. But India's dislike of formal treaties and alliances is genuine. Military pacts, Nehru once said, are 'a warlike approach to peace', and so he was critical of both CENTO and SEATO which touch tender spots on the periphery of Indian policy.

The Chinese attack on India's northern frontiers in the closing weeks of 1962 blew away a number of major illusions on which India's foreign policy had hitherto been sustained. It probably also shortened Nehru's life, for there is no doubt that he had sincerely desired, and believed in, China's friendship. He certainly gave no sign to the contrary. Perhaps for the first time since independence criticism came right out into the open, with the opposition Swatantra Party proclaiming an alternative foreign policy aimed at bringing India closer to the West. Indeed, the overall effect of the China episode was to knock Nehru's non-alignment policy off the fence on which it was uncertainly perched and to bring India nearer the USA and Britain, who alone among its friends came to its help at a moment when the country's military resources had reached a very low ebb indeed. At the same time India managed to retain good, even cordial, relations with Russia whom it regarded as an influential go-between with China, until the fierce ideological dispute broke out between Moscow and Peking. Though to the Chinese the border campaign is apparently a matter of secondary importance, it is viewed in a very different light by the Indians who, apart from the initial mortification of defeat, see themselves permanently threatened by their powerful adversary. In any event the affair assumed far bigger proportions than those of a border affray, to which some of India's critics would liken it.

On the whole, India's experiences during Nehru's years demonstrated that for purposes of evolving a practical foreign policy, it is not enough just to be on the side of freedom movements everywhere, or to condemn the atom and hydrogen bombs and the use of force generally, or to hold other estimable but highly generalised views. Concrete problems and situations require to be dealt with and, as we shall see, decisions have to be made often at very short notice.

Most leading statesmen have had considerable experience of the practical affairs of state by the time they reach their late fifties. Nehru had spent a working lifetime in strenuous political opposition, punctuated by jail sentences which amounted to more than ten years imprisonment in all. But it hardly needs saying that he brought to his high and responsible office a close knowledge of everything Indian and an immense love of his country, whose people gave him their full trust and confidence in return. Before the coming of the British, India was a congerie of territories each with its individual prince or ruler, and no man could remember the time when India, as India, had had a single Indian at the head of its government. But in 1947 the moment had come to restore to the Indian people both the symbols and reality of sovereign independence. No one who witnessed the rapturous events of those eventful days could have had the slightest doubt that the man they had chosen to epitomise India's new status was in every way worthy of the occasion. Jawaharlal Nehru was the first Indian ruler of the new India; his authority over his 400 million countrymen was unique and equalled only by that exercised by Mahatma Gandhi, and he stood aside from the daily business of government.

A number of theories have been put forward for Pandit Nehru's almost complete ascendancy during these many years over the Congress Party in the country and then in parliament, and over his colleagues in cabinet—not to mention the undisputed sway which he for so long exercised over the politically unattached masses of India. None of them is entirely convincing, and it is doubtful if there is any one explanation that is completely satisfying. Man must be regarded as a whole and rounded creature and, more than most, 'Panditji' demands to be seen and studied in the round if one is to understand his long and undisputed leadership of the Indian nation. It may sound trite, but it will bear saying that in

any setting he would have stood forth as an eminently noticeable person whom the casual stranger would inevitably pick
out as someone he wanted to know more about. For one thing,
he was a brahmin with all the unmistakable signs of intellectual fastidiousness which members of the caste seem to bear;
he was debonair and his good looks did not diminish with the
years. Until his last illness, he was not only lively and alert: he
was indefatigable; and for India he poured out his energy with
a rare prodigality. Yet none of these things—either singly or
together—accounts for his quite remarkable position in his own
country, where he was a prophet granted unique honour, or in
the neighbouring countries of South Asia which looked at
India and to Nehru for inspiration.

The Indian peasant lives and dies in poverty; the one sure
way to touch his heart is to show that you understand and are
willing (if only symbolically) to share his poverty with him.
Through the ages this has been the secret of the Hindu saints
and visionaries. Mahatma Gandhi understood this clearly, and
he elevated austerity to a ritual and extolled poverty as a
virtue. The Mahatma's influence on the Nehru family—
father and son alike—was indefinable but considerable. Quite
early in his political apprenticeship Pandit Nehru learnt to
identify himself with the poor of the Indian countryside and the
oppressed everywhere.

Those who knew him best are agreed that he saw no merit
in poverty for its own sake, and indeed as a practising socialist
desired that there should be plenty for everybody. In a posture
which combined human compassion with a practical political
ideal, he stood on the side of those who not only wished to be
'free' but who also, in a vague and ill articulated way, wanted
better material conditions of life. With the background of
Harrow, Cambridge and the Middle Temple, it would have
been easy to chose a rewarding professional career. Many
other decent and honourable men in his particular milieu in
Indian society chose to do so. In fact it was largely through
their mediation that the British Raj in India was able to
operate so smoothly for 150 years, and among them were not a
few of that small and select company of Kashmiri brahmins to
which the Nehru family belonged and who had settled in
northern India in the early eighteenth century.

So that, when he sought a place in the ranks of the Indian nationalist movement after the first world war, Jawaharlal Nehru clearly gave up many things which would, if he had wanted, have come to him easily and which other men might prize. He deliberately opted for an act of sacrifice; and in the instinctive way in which they seem to react, the Indian masses always felt that here was their man, and that he was prepared to do battle for them whatever the cost. But while ready to make all the sacrifices necessary, at the same time he removed from the politics of nationalism some of that odour of sanctity with which the Mahatma had invested them—though he would almost certainly have regarded any criticism of his master as being in the nature of *lèse majesté*.

It is important to remember this side of Nehru when one is tempted—as one sometimes is—to see only what seems to be impetuous or petulant or self-opinionated or unctuous in a man of very great qualities. One needs to remember that he came to office at an age when a good many men would be thinking that the moment had come to rest their oars; that he did not ride to the top on other people's backs but marched with them; and that, however nominal the Indian 'freedom struggle' may have been to some people, in one form or another it intensively filled thirty-five years of his life, leaving only a few short years (as such things are counted) for him to give effect to some of the things that he desired for India.

This book is an attempt to make a provisional estimate of Nehru's success or otherwise in implementing his policies during the years of supreme authority after 1947, to furnish the reader with a pro-forma statement of account and to strike, as it were, a trial balance. For this purpose we shall need amongst other things to take a fairly close look at Nehru's concept of economic planning, for in the field of planning India's successes and failures have had a considerable influence on the rest of the developing world. Happily, not all the underdeveloped countries are in the grip of a population explosion as violent as India's, but undoubtedly many of the difficulties which beset it today have their genesis in this. What, if anything, is being done about it? Apart from his position as the head of Government, we shall consider Pandit Nehru in his various other roles:

as foreign minister, as party leader, as minister responsible for
Atomic Development, as Commonwealth and world statesman.
And finally we must ask what his contribution to the unity of
India has been. These are some of the questions that will be
posed. It is unlikely that we will be able to pass a final verdict
on all or any of them; but we know enough to form a worthwhile provisional judgement.

2

UNDERWRITING THE PLANS

NATIONALISM AND SOCIALISM were the intellectual driving forces of Nehru's life work, and of these nationalism was by far the most powerful for most of the time. During the period of his education, economics did not rate very high as an academic subject, in spite of the fact that the great Marshall was radiating light and learning from Nehru's own University of Cambridge. His socialism developed gradually and, as befitted his cast of mind, was Fabian rather than Marxist. His approach to economic problems was essentially 'pragmatic', to use a favourite adjective of his. For him socialism seemed the only economic creed which was compatible with the Indian freedom struggle; a large part of Indian capitalism was associated with alien rule and for that reason if for no other stood condemned. It is not suggested that Nehru's socialism was built wholly upon quite such a simple philosophy as this, but clearly it would have been very difficult for a man who was so distinctively a product of his own aristocratic background and of western European liberalism to combine with the liberation movement a policy of 'no change' on the economic front.

It is significant that the three top leaders of the Congress Party—Mahatma Gandhi, Sardar Patel and Pandit Nehru—who more than any other three men may be said to have steered India to freedom, differed widely in their views as to the way the economy of independent India could best be organised. The Mahatma was profoundly distrustful of the large units of a machine-based urban economy and believed that Indian industry should be directly linked to the country's 700,000

B

villages, the spinning wheel and whatever else could be employed with reasonable efficiency in the home. His was a sort of William Morris vision of the future. Sardar Patel, who in his lifetime had witnessed the rise and triumph of the Bombay and Ahmedabad cotton mill companies, saw nothing wrong (and indeed a great deal that was right and proper) in mass production by factory methods and all the other attributes of modern capitalism. Nehru was for socialism.

But, though his writings leave no doubt as to which economic system he favoured, before and after he assumed office as prime minister of India, Nehru's approach to matters calling for economic judgements was tentative and gradual. Two examples will suffice. The socialist trend of his writings in the early and middle 1930s undoubtedly had great influence on those younger members of the Congress Party who, under the leadership of Jai Prakash Narayan, founded the Congress Socialist Party in 1934. Much to their disappointment, however, Nehru never joined this party within a party, though he was several times pressed to do so. Whether he thought it would prejudice his larger loyalty to Congress, or whether, as some observers think, he regarded the particular CSP brand of socialism as too doctrinaire for Indian conditions, is not clear. But the fact is that he declined formal membership of the party.

The other example is his sponsorship at the Avadi session of the National Congress Party of the formula of 'a Socialist Pattern of Society' as the goal of Indian policy.* A moment's

* Properly speaking, there were two policy resolutions on the subject of 'the Socialist Pattern' at the 60th annual session of the Indian National Congress held at Avadi, near Madras, on January 20, 1955. The first, standing in the name of Maulana Abul Kalam Azad, stated that the public sector of the economy must play a progressively greater part, more particularly in establishing the basic industries, while the private sector would continue to be important for other reasons. This resolution envisaged that planning should take place with a view to creating a 'socialistic pattern of society where the principal means of production is progressively speeded up and there is equitable distribution of national wealth'. The second resolution, moved by Nehru, said that in view of this declared objective the state would necessarily play a vital part in planning and development. 'In particular it will (1) initiate and operate large scale schemes providing services such as power, transport, etc; (2) have overall control of resources, social purposes and trends and essential balances in the economy; (3) check and prevent the evils of anarchic industrial development by the

thought makes it clear that the pursuit of a socialist pattern as the aim of policy is likely to turn out to be a substantially different thing from the pursuit of a socialist policy. And so it has proved, in spite of the dark fears entertained in the Indian business world at the time. The Avadi resolution was in fact an umbrella under which the catholicity and predictable contradictions of Nehru's patently sincere, but highly flexible, socialist philosophy could be equally comfortably accommodated. 'Why was this decision for a socialist pattern of society taken', he rhetorically asked the Federation of Indian Chambers of Commerce in a speech on March 5, 1955. 'It was taken to give an indication of the objective and approach. We have to fit India into the nuclear age and do it quickly. . . . All the factors that have conditioned India have to be remembered.' This statement is typical of Nehru's bland and baffling treatment of economic questions. *Ex parte* we are asked to assume that the socialist pattern of society is, firstly, the only way by which India can be quickly fitted into the new nuclear world order; and secondly, that it is the only economic system that will take proper account of India's past. To put it mildly, this is claiming rather too much for the 'socialist pattern'.

The real test—and the one by which presumably Nehru would wish to be judged—is not whether India has been enabled to embrace socialism, but whether in his years in power he laid the groundwork for the conversion of her economy into that of a modern state. Nehru was impatient of delays and ardently desired change, but it was too much to expect that in the relatively short period of seventeen years he could do more than lay the foundations of a new economical and social structure in a country in which the vast majority of its 430 million inhabitants lived and died in extreme poverty and abysmal ignorance. In the long perspective of history, and from the point of view of the Indian people, it matters little whether Nehru's policies have followed the strict letter of socialism. What matters for them is whether his policies have succeeded in getting the economy moving upwards and have created conditions in which the peoples' standard of living is

maintenance of strategic controls, prevention of private trusts and cartels and the maintenance of standards of labour and production; (4) plan the economy of the nation in its basic and broad aspects.'

rising, and both national and per capita income is increasing
faster than the population is growing.

Nehru was very conscious of the desperate poverty of the
great majority of his fellow countrymen. He did not accept
that it was inevitable or that nothing could be done about
it; in his view the state had a duty actively to intervene if its
subjects were oppressed by the economic conditions under
which they lived. This duty is specifically enshrined in Article
39 of Part IV of the Indian Constitution, whose Directive
Principles include an obligation to ensure:

(a) that the citizens, men and women equally, have the right
to adequate means of livelihood;

(b) that the ownership and control of the material resources
of the community are so distributed as best to subserve the
common good; and

(c) that the operation of the economic system does not
result in the concentration of wealth and means of production
to the common detriment.

For the purpose of controlling the direction and promoting the
growth of the Indian economy, Nehru chose the Five Year
Plan as his chief regulatory weapon. Though he had for long
been attracted to the idea of economic planning as the means
by which the state could ensure the fullest development of the
nation's resources, he did not straight away plunge into a
complicated planning exercise immediately on taking office in
1947. There were other and more pressing matters demanding
his attention, and furthermore it seemed as though he was, for
the time being, watching the current performance of the
economy before making up his mind to try to accelerate its
growth rate. This pause for reflection undoubtedly gave the
wrong impression in some business and industrial circles who
were misled into thinking that, notwithstanding the vast
political changes that had taken place, the economy would
run on in much the same fashion as before. The Indian parliament's first Industrial Policy Resolution of April 6, 1948, with
its three categories of enterprise—those reserved exclusively
for the state, those in which the state and privately owned

units could coexist, and the much larger third classification in which private enterprise would be allowed a clear field—gave little support to the idea that Nehru was contemplating an industrial revolution or the wholesale nationalisation of the means of production and distribution. Nor was he.

Indeed, Nehru's economic policies are best understood if one thinks of his socialism as being of a rather tentative and experimental kind. He was too sensitive and humane to be of the stuff of which revolutionaries are made and, given the choice his instinct was to improve the system rather than to abolish it. In his later years, his declared attitude to wealth was sometimes harsh and unreasonably indignant, but that was because he saw it against the contrasting background of India's all-pervading poverty. He was critical of the private enterprise system because it appeared to him to accept the poverty of the masses as part of the natural order, and indeed to a large extent to subsist on it. The fact was that he had no close understanding of how the private sector works and, in spite of his great intellectual gifts, he had an imperfect acquaintance with the functioning of the economic machine as a whole. With the exception of a few brief years when he practised at the Bar as a junior to his father, his whole mature and working life was devoted to politics. He took no interest in business and (so far as this writer knows) had no business friends, his intimates being chiefly drawn from political, professional and intellectual circles. But if Jawaharlal Nehru had no detailed knowledge of the machinery of the Indian economy, he certainly knew what he wanted it to do.

A small Planning Department had been set up in the last years of the British administration, but it was not until March 1950 that the Planning Commission of independent India was created—two and a half years after independence—and we may suppose that the interval was partly occupied by thinking out the position. As the fanciful suggestion has been made of a 'strike' of capital* soon after Nehru took office, it is important

* See, for example, *Nehru: A Political Biography*, by Michael Brecher, 1959. Chapter XII of this most readable study says the real problem in 1948 was a crisis in business confidence 'now that Nehru was Prime Minister. Insecurity led to a "strike of capital" pending the announcement of the Government's industrial policy.'

to appreciate just what the situation i...
particular time.

India had ended the war with a heavily...
in which important manufacturing indu...
cotton) were severed from their main sou...
by the partition of the subcontinent. For...
the transport system had been grossly over...
of the Allied war effort and was seriously...
Bengal famine had exposed the extreme...
food supplies which stood between the...
starvation. To add to a long list of other t...
which for fifty years had been a major...
petroleum—was now completely out of...
exporter of either because of war deva...
worst of the refugee movements were over...
moved across the Indian border and the p...
tion and resettlement remained to be dealt...
the war from credits for goods and ser...
Allied forces in the eastern theatres, In...
stood at an all-time high, but because of...
capital goods (and many consumer goods t...
spent for some time to come. Wartime...
stock and share quotations to record hei...
budget of the Interim Government, in w...
Liaquat Ali Khan held the Finance portfoli...
on the Indian stock exchanges the like o...
seen before or since. Not a few wartime...
overnight, and more than one observer r...
proposals as a deliberate thrust at the...
Hindus, of which Moslem India was tradit...
For eighteen months after this event, capit...
strike' as sorely stricken.

Such were some of the more prominent...
mic scene which confronted Nehru on ta...
India's first completely independent admi...
certainly not such as to encourage a spir...
or the adoption of new and untried ideas...
case for leaving excursions into socialism...
moment.

It will perhaps be helpful if at this poin...

units could coexist, and the much larger third classification in which private enterprise would be allowed a clear field—gave little support to the idea that Nehru was contemplating an industrial revolution or the wholesale nationalisation of the means of production and distribution. Nor was he.

Indeed, Nehru's economic policies are best understood if one thinks of his socialism as being of a rather tentative and experimental kind. He was too sensitive and humane to be of the stuff of which revolutionaries are made and, given the choice his instinct was to improve the system rather than to abolish it. In his later years, his declared attitude to wealth was sometimes harsh and unreasonably indignant, but that was because he saw it against the contrasting background of India's all-pervading poverty. He was critical of the private enterprise system because it appeared to him to accept the poverty of the masses as part of the natural order, and indeed to a large extent to subsist on it. The fact was that he had no close understanding of how the private sector works and, in spite of his great intellectual gifts, he had an imperfect acquaintance with the functioning of the economic machine as a whole. With the exception of a few brief years when he practised at the Bar as a junior to his father, his whole mature and working life was devoted to politics. He took no interest in business and (so far as this writer knows) had no business friends, his intimates being chiefly drawn from political, professional and intellectual circles. But if Jawaharlal Nehru had no detailed knowledge of the machinery of the Indian economy, he certainly knew what he wanted it to do.

A small Planning Department had been set up in the last years of the British administration, but it was not until March 1950 that the Planning Commission of independent India was created—two and a half years after independence—and we may suppose that the interval was partly occupied by thinking out the position. As the fanciful suggestion has been made of a 'strike' of capital* soon after Nehru took office, it is important

---

* See, for example, *Nehru: A Political Biography*, by Michael Brecher, 1959. Chapter XII of this most readable study says the real problem in 1948 was a crisis in business confidence 'now that Nehru was Prime Minister. Insecurity led to a "strike of capital" pending the announcement of the Government's industrial policy.'

to appreciate just what the situation in India was at this particular time.

India had ended the war with a heavily overloaded economy in which important manufacturing industries (e.g. jute and cotton) were severed from their main sources of raw materials by the partition of the subcontinent. For more than four years the transport system had been grossly overworked in the interest of the Allied war effort and was seriously run down. The 1943 Bengal famine had exposed the extremely narrow margin of food supplies which stood between the country and sheer starvation. To add to a long list of other tribulations, Burma—which for fifty years had been a major supplier of rice and petroleum—was now completely out of the running as an exporter of either because of war devastation. Though the worst of the refugee movements were over, a steady stream still moved across the Indian border and the problem of rehabilitation and resettlement remained to be dealt with. Built up during the war from credits for goods and services supplied to the Allied forces in the eastern theatres, India's foreign reserves stood at an all-time high, but because of a world shortage of capital goods (and many consumer goods too) they could not be spent for some time to come. Wartime inflation had carried stock and share quotations to record heights, but the 1947–8 budget of the Interim Government, in which the late Nawab Liaquat Ali Khan held the Finance portfolio, produced a collapse on the Indian stock exchanges the like of which has not been seen before or since. Not a few wartime fortunes disappeared overnight, and more than one observer regarded the Nawab's proposals as a deliberate thrust at the money power of the Hindus, of which Moslem India was traditionally apprehensive. For eighteen months after this event, capital was not so much 'on strike' as sorely stricken.

Such were some of the more prominent features of the economic scene which confronted Nehru on taking office as head of India's first completely independent administration. They were certainly not such as to encourage a spirit of experimentation or the adoption of new and untried ideas. There was a strong case for leaving excursions into socialism for a more propitious moment.

It will perhaps be helpful if at this point we set down a brief chronology of the evolution of Nehru's economic policy for India as revealed in the early years of independence. The main signposts are:

1. *1948:* The creation of a Mixed Economy is indicated by the first Industrial Policy Resolution which divided Indian industry into three categories, i.e. those whose ownership and management are reserved to the state, those in which the state and private enterprise can coexist and those in which private enterprise is free to operate, subject to some official controls.

2. *1950:* The establishment of a National Planning Commission and the publication in July 1951 of the draft outline of the First Five Year Plan (1951–6), with targets for both the public and private sectors, indicating that henceforth planning by a central authority was to be the chief agency for economic development.

3. *1955 :* The adoption by the ruling Congress Party of a resolution that the attainment of a 'socialist pattern of society' was to be the goal of all policy.

4. *1956*: A second official Industrial Policy Resolution carried Nehru's socialist philosophy somewhat further, declaring: 'The adoption of the socialist pattern of society as the national objective, as well as the need for planned and rapid development, requires that all industries of basic and strategic importance, or in the nature of public utility services, should be in the public sector. Other industries which are on a scale which only the state, in present circumstances, could provide, have also to be in the public sector. The state has therefore to assume direct responsibility for the future development of industries over a wider area.'

Neither state-ownership nor the idea of planning was entirely unknown in pre-independent India, which had been ahead of Britain and some other European countries in having a nationalised railway system. Virtually the whole of its 35,000 miles of railways were state-owned by the 1930s and with it a sizeable complex of engineering workshops and collieries. Government exercised a complete monopoly over salt and opium manufacture and the making of armaments. It had stepped in and

bought up a languishing privately owned radio network and
had established a national broadcasting system which, at the
time, was superior to that of most other Asian countries. The
old government of India was, in fact, quite a substantial trader
on its own account and had as much experience of operating
commercial departments as other governments—and more than
most. But, of course, it was not state-ownership of this kind
that the Industrial Policy Resolutions had in mind, or that
would fit into the socialist pattern visualised by Congress,
which clearly desired the acquisition of important basic
industries.

Pandit Nehru had long been personally interested in economic planning, having been much impressed by what he saw
during a visit to Soviet Russia in 1927. He studied the first
Soviet Five Year Plan in some detail. In 1938 Congress had
set up a Planning Committee with Nehru as its chairman. It
produced a series of reports and plans of various kinds which
today possess no more than historical interest. This was planning *in vacuo*, though it implanted the seeds of ideas which were
to germinate into concrete schemes later. More recently, in
1944, the idea of a planned economy had been given a fillip and
some publicity by the issue of a document known as the Bombay
Plan. This was a scheme for the expansion of the Indian
economy (mainly by widening its industrial base), prepared by
and published over the signature of a dozen or so well known
Indian industrialists including such eminent business leaders as
J. R. D. Tata, G. D. Birla, Sir Homi Mody, the late N. R.
Sarker and others. The Bombay Plan was presented to the
country as the rough outline of an economic programme
which was to cost Rs 10,000 crores* (£7,500 million). Its chief
merit was that it focused public attention on India's needs and,
by reason of the distinguished auspices under which it was put
forward, it implied the commitment of the Indian business
community to the principle of planned economic growth. There
is no evidence that Nehru ever regarded the Bombay Plan very
seriously, but he doubtless took due note of the fact that the
leaders of Indian trade and industry had pledged their support
for the national economic plan.

* A crore is 10 million rupees and is equal to £750,000 or $2,100,000. Rs
1 lakh, which is equivalent to 100,000 rupees, is equal to £7,500.

Thus, when the details of the First Five Year Plan were announced, it was to a public whose mind had been well conditioned to planning. The only thing out of the ordinary was the seemingly astronomical dimensions of the sums of money involved. After some initial haggling, the total of the various allocations in the Plan was fixed at Rs 2,378 crores ($£1,783\frac{1}{2}$ million), outlay amounting to Rs 2,013 crores ($£1,509\frac{3}{4}$ million). Annual Plan expenditure rose from Rs 256 crores in the financial year 1951–2 to Rs 666 crores in 1955–6. These are sums which we would regard as commonplace today, but in 1951 they seemed gargantuan. The multiplier effect was asserting itself with a vengeance, yet the results were pitifully meagre, and at this level of investment it was obviously going to be a very long time before planning made even the mildest dent in India's chronic problems of poverty, unemployment and disease. Nehru had signified his personal involvement in economic planning by becoming chairman of the Planning Commission and as such was the titular head of the economic general staff, sharing with other ministers responsibility to parliament and the country for the scope and working of the Plan. In the circumstances, the choice of a whole-time deputy chairman was important, for upon him devolved supervision of the detailed work of the Commission. For this first appointment it was necessary to find someone who was an expositor as well as a reliable rather than impetuous planner. Nehru accordingly went outside the ranks of the professional administrators, whom he suspected to be not very receptive of new ideas and therefore not the best people to 'sell' such things to those authorities on whose co-operation the success of the Plan depended. He chose G. L. Mehta of the Scindia Shipping Company, later India's ambassador in Washington— a public man who combined a successful business career with a respectable academic record, and with talents as a speaker and a writer. Both the size of the Plan and its scope were well within India's capacity to manage and in the end the chief criticism of it was that it was not ambitious enough and was too modest in its aims.

But Nehru and his advisers undoubtedly knew what they were doing. They considered it would be unwise to superimpose, upon all the other strains involved with independence and partition, a Five Year Plan which would place an insupportable burden on the economy. The targets set by the First Five Year Plan were comfortably realised, and the ease with which this was accomplished bred a measure of confidence in planning in both the administration and the public which no amount of propaganda would have accomplished. In fact, it probably made economic planning appear altogether too easy. A series of good harvests meant that there was practically no curb on current consumption, while India's substantial external reserves ensured that trade and industry were still free of the cramping effects of a foreign exchange shortage. The central purpose of the First Plan was defined as initiating 'a process of development which will raise living standards and open out to the people new opportunities for a richer and more varied life'. These are the beneficent objectives of all good government, and it can reasonably be argued that India did not need a £1,500 million plan to formulate them. What it did require, however, was a restatement of faith to mark the inauguration of the new chapter of history that had begun in 1947. As well as fresh economic techniques, the country also needed new hope for the future. Nobody understood this better than Pandit Nehru, and nobody was better able to put India's aspirations into words.

Before considering in more detail the three Five Year Plans launched during the Nehru regime, a word must be said about the philosophy of Indian planning and the organisation of its machinery, both of which were much influenced in their early stages by Nehru's thinking. At the apex of the planning structure stands the National Planning Commission, presided over by the prime minister, and whose membership also includes the finance minister and the minister for planning. The role of the deputy chairman has already been mentioned. In addition to him there are a number of advisers and other senior functionaries, including a liberal sprinkling of economists and statisticians. Through the ministers close contact is maintained with cabinet and parliament, while the governments of the States are brought into the picture by means of the National Development Council on which they are represented by their chief ministers and development commissioners. The National

Development Council meets twice or more in a year, and non-official professional experience is drawn from periodical meetings of standing panels of scientists and economists.

The Planning Commission has no executive powers, but obviously it can and does exercise very considerable influence. It ties together the various central and States' development schemes (or at least those of which it approves); it sanctions modernisation and expansion plans for whole industries and trading groups; it has a big voice in determining the fields in which growth shall be encouraged; it fixes production and other targets and it prepares the massive documents in which the texts of the Five Year Plans are enshrined—and much else besides. In practice the Commission has a voice in all economic decision-making at some point in the long chain of responsi- bility. It is almost, but not quite, as powerful as the Finance Ministry itself.

The other point to be noted is that, from the beginning, Nehru sought to make the process of consultation as wide and comprehensive as possible. At an early stage each Five Year Plan was, as it were, thrown open for public debate. This is what distinguishes planning in a democracy from planning in a totalitarian state, and the large element of 'consent' upon which Indian planning methods and objectives depend is one of the features which sharply differentiate the Indian Five Year Plans from similar exercises in the Communist countries. From the point of view of the technocrat who wants to get things done, and who measures his success chiefly by the speed with which a bridge is built or a steel works gets into production or a satellite into orbit, the authoritarian method of planning has its advan- tages. But for those who believe that the people should under- stand, and as far as possible participate in, the decisions and actions of government (and Nehru held strongly to such beliefs), planning by consent is the only way of managing a phased programme of development.

From this point of view, the Indian experiment has been of crucial importance to the whole of the free, democratic world. It would, of course, be quite impossible to submit every detail of every Five Year Plan to the Indian parliament for its approval, though eventually parliament does approve such plans *in toto*. But it has been the practice that, as a plan is being

pieced together and built up, opinion on its contents and feasibility is sought from as many quarters as possible, even at the
cost of some operational delay. Quite apart from the Planning
Commission itself (and its associated bodies such as the National
Development Council), trade and industrial associations,
chambers of commerce, trade unions and other organs of non-
official opinion are consulted on the main projects and purposes
of the plan, with the result that at every stage public opinion is
pretty well informed of the government's intentions.

Nor are facilities for inspection and criticism restricted to
individuals and organisations within the country. India must
be one of the most publicised and 'written about' countries in
the world today: a circumstance which is very largely due to
its Five Year Plans and to the policy of encouraging economists,
scientists, writers, politicians *et hoc genus omne* everywhere to
come and see for themselves what is going on. This policy was
actively supported by Pandit Nehru, with the result that
India's problems and the achievements of its development
plans have become known to an ever enlarging world public,
particularly in the West, from which the country draws much
of its external assistance. Foreign economists enjoying long
periods of sabbatical leave have visited the country in substantial numbers; financial journalists have made long tours
of investigation; the planning machine both at the centre and
in the States has been thrown open for searching inspection.
The number of doctoral and other higher degrees theses which
have been written about the Indian economy must be legion.
Not all the comment has been favourable, but no one (either
foreign or Indian) who has written in criticism of the Indian
plans has been penalised for his opinions. Unhappily, the same
cannot be said of some other developing countries.

This tolerant and enlightened attitude is in no small measure
due to Pandit Nehru who, though impatient in some matters,
was never afraid of honest criticism in public affairs. So far as
the Planning Commission is concerned, his example has been
followed at all levels of the organisation. There is no doubt that
this frank method of revealing the progress (or otherwise) of the
Five Year Plans has done much to inspire confidence in the
Indian record. It shows the country in a favourable light by
comparison with, for example, China—concerning whose

economic affairs it is extremely difficult to obtain any kind of reliable data. Furthermore, the Finance Ministry, the Reserve Bank of India and the Planning Commission are amongst the best documented institutions outside Europe and North America. This makes it easier to get at the facts on which judgements can be made.

In the foregoing pages an attempt has been made to describe something of the spirit informing Indian economic planning —which carries in many ways the clear impress of Nehru's personality. In the next chapter we go on to consider the plans themselves. Planners are prone to think that they alone can prescribe the remedies for the great economic maladies which they are trying to cure. Naturally, they know more than most people about what is, after all, their field of specialisation. But Nehru never accepted that planning was only for planners; in India, at least, it was something to which everybody could contribute and he was quite as willing to listen to the head of a village *panchayat* as he was to discuss some current planning problem with an Indian or foreign expert. Perhaps because his own knowledge of economic matters was not very profound he was the more willing to garner the opinions of others. This democratisation of the processes of planning led some of his leftwing critics to regard him as a sort of lapsed socialist who had lost his faith in the pure doctrine of collectivism. That his hope lay chiefly in people rather than in things was poignantly recorded in his last will and testament, in which he directed that his ashes should be carried high in an aircraft and scattered 'over the fields where the peasants of India toil, so that they might mingle with the dust and soil of India and become an indistinguishable part of her'.

3

THE MALTHUSIAN
DILEMMA

THE SUMMER OF 1965 saw India plunged into the latest of the dozen food crises with which the country has been afflicted since 1943. It might be said that it is rather poor testimony to economic planning if, after nearly fifteen years, it cannot provide India's inhabitants with the assurance of one square meal a day. But the picture is not quite as simple and straightforward as many people in the West seem to imagine. Nehru himself had told the National Development Council in 1957: 'We had rather an easy time in the First Five Year Plan, because really we had not stretched ourselves. We had not made any particular effort. We just took what there was and called it a Plan.' Though somewhat of an exaggeration, this deprecatory confession was true in substance. A large part of the First Five Year Plan was a collation and systematisation of schemes which, in some cases, had been in existence for quite a time. Targets were prescribed for important categories of production, and the idea of cumulative economic growth was set before the country, which for the first time began to hear its government talking in terms of growth indices, 'take-off' theories and national income statistics. The intellectual Hindu is a serious minded person, and the vision of a planned economy which was now beginning to emerge quickly fired the imagination of the educated classes—particularly the young men and women of the towns and cities of India. This, they said, was something worth backing. Nehru had not only won India its freedom: it now seemed he also knew what the country should do with it.

But, of course, economic plans are not always to be equated with economic performance. The First Five Year Plan reached most of its targets comfortably, and if it did not materially change the face of the Indian economy it was because it was not big enough for a job that is likely to take nearer fifty than five years to complete. Without realising it, India operated the First Plan under circumstances a good deal more favourable than it might ordinarily have expected or has experienced since. Furthermore, partly by accident but mostly by design, the physical goals which India set itself were well within its staying power. The result was a passing economic euphoria. Nonetheless this had its uses in that it afforded the planning machine a trial run, enabled the planners to acquire a measure of practical experience and gave the country a sense of achievement. The self-confidence thus engendered was to prove useful in the more difficult days of the Second and Third Plans which lay ahead.

Figures have been given in the previous chapter of the total First Plan allocations (Rs 2,378 crores) and of the estimated outlay which fell short of the allocations by around Rs 400 crores. (The reader is warned that, owing to the leads and lags in plan expenditure and receipts, and items carried over from one five-year period to another, it is often very difficult to give precise totals for the various heads of Indian planning.) Today the arithmetic of the First Plan is of little more than academic interest, except for the prime fact that it set the rough pattern which was to govern the financial arrangements for subsequent plans. Deficit financing (Rs 420 crores) was to provide more than 20 per cent of the Rs. 1,960 crores' worth of expenditure actually incurred in the First Five Year Plan. In such a situation it was obvious that inflation was the major danger which the country had to guard against. In having recourse to credit creation on the scale contemplated, Nehru and his colleagues were taking a grave though finely calculated risk. But it came off. Prices at the end of the plan were lower by 13 per cent than they had been when the plan started; in fact, they were slightly below the level at which they had stood on the eve of the Korean war, from which India did not benefit nearly as much as some other primary producers. Throughout 1955 the all-India cost-of-living index averaged 96 compared with 100 in 1949. Money-supply in the hands of the public at the close of the fiscal year 1955–6 (effectively the last year of the First Plan) was about Rs 208 crores above the level of early 1951, when the plan started. This was an increase of a little over 10 per cent compared with an estimated increase of some 18 per cent in national income. The Reserve Bank's holdings of foreign securities, together with the balances it keeps abroad, rose from Rs 723·07 crores in 1951–2 to Rs 746·14 crores in 1955–6, this being the last period of years over which India's external reserves registered a small but progressive increase. At the end of the First Plan, the Planning Commission were able to report: 'Domestic inflationary pressures in several countries are at present probably stronger than in India where there is more confidence and greater readiness all round for a larger effort.'

The First Plan, in fact, went through to completion without disturbance to key points of the economy. In the five years from 1951 to 1956 Indian per capita income recorded an increase of 10·5 per cent; investment in the public and private sectors of the economy came up to expectations; industrial and agricultural production was both diversified and increased; and social overhead capital, in one form or another, was significantly added to. As the plan unfolded it was clear there was something in it for everybody—or almost everybody. Agricultural production rose steadily and the 1955–6 output of foodgrains (64·8 million tons) was more than 10 per cent up since the beginning of the plan. This was pleasing news to those who continued to argue that agriculture ought to be given first priority in what was essentially an agricultural country. Large-scale power and irrigation schemes, in many instances already well in hand before the inauguration of the plan, were designed to help agriculture and industry equally. Industrial production increased overall by nearly 40 per cent, the biggest advances being made in established lines like cotton textiles, jute manufactures, sugar and so on. This was something to bring joy to the hearts of those many others who maintained that India was now in a position to take a tremendous leap forward.

The Planning Commission estimated that new fixed investment in the private sector of industry during the First Plan amounted to Rs 340 crores (£255 million). This substantial sum was fairly evenly spread over a wide range of manufacturing and extractive activities. In the public (i.e. state-owned) sector of industry, the government—with no firm preconceived ideas in mind—was testing the possibilities and had already made a beginning in the manufacture of fertilisers, newsprint, penicillin, cables, telephones, machine tools and locomotives. This was a very mixed assortment with no very logical pattern. For instance, the government found itself a manufacturer of newsprint by pure accident rather than as a deliberate act of policy. A sum of Rs 101 crores had been proposed for spending during the period of the plan on the public ownership of industrial projects. In actual fact an investment of not more than Rs 60 crores had been made by the end of the First Plan, from which it may reasonably be inferred that at this stage the government was not exactly burning with zeal to go into the business of manufacturing on its own account. On the other hand, it had begun to examine basic industrial requirements. An expansion scheme for the small state-owned Mysore Iron and Steel Works had been put in hand, and preparatory planning had begun for three public-sector steel plants, each of one million tons ingot capacity, which were later to become the centrepiece of the Second Five Year Plan.

At this juncture two points may be noted: first, largely as a result of the Congress Party 'Socialist Pattern' resolution at Avadi in 1955, state ownership and trading had taken on a new urgency in official thinking; secondly, planning was being increasingly directed to increasing the supply of indigenous steel as the basis for further industrial development. The effects of these trends would be seen later.

Yet, convincing as they may have seemed at the time, some of the successes of the First Plan were to prove illusory. The planners had not really taken the measure of the two points at which India was most vulnerable, viz, food and population—factors which, in any case, are inextricably mixed up with one another. In spite of the vast extension of irrigation facilities in the subcontinent over the past sixty years or so, 80 per cent of India's cultivated land still depends on the annual monsoon rain rather than stored water. A poor monsoon means poor crops, and trouble all round for everybody from the finance minister down to the humblest peasant. A failure of the monsoon may well bring in its wake famine, death and desolation. At its grass roots the economy is always at the caprice of the monsoon. India usually has too much or too little water; it is the purpose of a balanced irrigation system to even out supplies, so that the cultivator has enough water to meet the exigencies of a poor monsoon. So far, the administration has not succeeded in creating this stage of equilibrium.

But a government is entitled to some of the luck of the weather, and it so happened that the early and middle 1950s were blessed by a series of good monsoons, resulting in exceptionally good harvests; so much so that imports of foodgrains which had reached 4.73 million tons in 1950 had fallen to less than a million tons in 1955 and 1956. This was of immense psychological and practical value and the Second Plan Outline, reflecting the official thinking of the time, attributed the happy state of affairs to the increased use of fertilisers, new minor irrigation works, better quality seeds and community development schemes—in other words, to the beneficent influence of the First Plan. No doubt all of these things played some part in boosting agricultural output, but the inescapable fact is that the chief contributor to the improvement was the weather. And it is to be feared that, by giving insufficient credit to the good weather and too much credit to miscellaneous items of rural development, the planners and politicians tended to mask the real situation, which was and is that for its food India works to the smallest margin of safety; that food supplies are precariously balanced on a knife-edge, on one side of which is a perpetual condition of shortage and on the other a growing number of men, women and children to feed as each year goes by. The Indian government is thus constantly faced by a grim malthusian dilemma, which in 1964 prompted the deputy chairman of the Planning Commission, Asoka Mehta, to call for the sterilisation of a million Indian males a year until further notice.

There had been a census of undivided India, conducted under wartime conditions, in 1941; ten years later, in 1951, India had its first census as an independent sovereign state in occupation of a part, but not the whole, of the subcontinent.

The counting of heads—and the inferences (present and future) to be made from the figures so collected—was going on at the same time as the First Five Year Plan was being prepared. It is doubtful if the authors of the latter took sufficient account of the incremental factor which has made India's population growth one of the most explosive in the world. The first plan assumed a population growth rate of 1·25 per cent per annum for twenty years from 1951. It was not long before it was realised that this was a considerable underestimate, and steps were taken in the Second Plan Outline to correct this too comfortable assumption and replace it with a more realistic growth rate. Based on the data provided by the next decennial census (1961), the rate of growth of India's population is now assumed to be 2·4 or 2·5 per cent.

The population question must recur many times in any consideration of the Nehru years; it is mentioned now because it is closely bound up with the subject of 'new employment opportunities', in the creation of which the First Five Year Plan had fallen a good deal short of the hopes of its authors. Full employment, in the sense in which the term is used in the West, is unhappily unattainable in the India of today—and will probably be so for a good many years to come. The most that the initial series of plans can be expected to do is to create some new kinds of employment and the basic growth conditions in which men and women will increasingly find useful work to do. The effect of a programme of industrialisation should be to create employment opportunities of a non-agricultural character.

But 'employment opportunities' is itself rather a nebulous term which is not susceptible to precise definition or measurement. There is no evidence that the First Five Year Plan made any particular impact in this crucial department of planning; on the contrary there is some evidence to support the theory that urban unemployment (which is mostly responsive to rough measurement devices) grew somewhat worse between 1951 and 1956. Using the admittedly very inadequate data provided by the scattered urban labour exchanges, at which it is thought that about a quarter of all unemployed in the cities and towns of India register themselves, the Planning Commission estimated urban unemployment to be around 2¼ million in

1954—almost certainly an underestimate. On the other hand
the Commission claim that 'direct employment generated
during the first plan period in the public and private sectors
was of the order of 4·5 million'. So the inquirer has a wide
range of choice on which to form a judgement. Unemployment
and underemployment merge into one another, and there is no
clear dividing line between the two. Is an Indian peasant who
spends five months out of the year tending his land to be
regarded as constantly underemployed, or as unemployed for
seven months out of twelve? His condition is unenviable which-
ever way one looks at it and it has to be said that the First
Plan had only a slight influence on the problem.

Very sensibly, neither Nehru nor his advisers claimed more for
the First Five Year Plan than the facts would justify. It could
be held against them that, in the light of recent history, they
were a bit too complacent over the food problem and that they
failed to grasp the grim possibilities of the rise in population
which had been seriously underestimated by the demographers.
They failed to see that the population question was an integral
part of the development problem and not something distinct
from it, or something which could wait until later on. Yet
today we speak and write with the advantage of hindsight. In
1955 most observers thought India had done well to carry
through a fair-sized development programme without a breakdown. There was plenty of evidence of accelerating economic
activity and an infectious air of optimism. India had shown
that it had the capacity to become, in due course, a major
industrial country, and that in addition it might well set the
pattern for an Asian version of the welfare state. Much of the
credit for all this went to Nehru personally. Though it was not
his responsibility to look after the details of economic development—and indeed he was sometimes more than a little vague
about some of them—it was he who provided the vision and
the drive and in a very real sense was the focal point from which
radiated much of the enthusiasm for planning. He let it be
known that the Second Five Year Plan was to be a considerably
more ambitious affair, one which would call for a much bigger
national and individual effort.

Work on the Second Plan began in April 1954, and a first

draft was submitted to the National Development Council in May 1955. In their preamble to the final draft the Planning Commission said: 'Our Second Five Year Plan seeks to re-build rural India, to lay the foundations of industrial progress and to secure to the greatest extent feasible opportunities for the weaker and underprivileged sections of our people and the balanced development of all parts of the country.' Noble language worthy of a great project, but not easy to translate into action. The first draft also made a more serious attempt to define what was meant by a socialist pattern of society. It insisted that in such a pattern 'the basic criterion for determining the lines of advance must be not private profit but social gain', while 'major decisions regarding production, distribution, consumption and investment—in fact all significant socio-economic relationships—must be made by agencies informed by social purpose'. With the message of Avadi obviously fresh in their thoughts, the planners said 'the organisation and management of public enterprises is a field in which considerable experimentation will be necessary and this holds, in fact, for the entire socialist pattern'. Within these terms of reference the Second Five Year Plan had as specific objectives:

1. A sizeable increase in national income so as to raise the level of living in the country;

2. Rapid industrialisation, with particular emphasis on the development of basic and heavy industries;

3. A large expansion of employment opportunities;

4. Reduction of inequalities in income and wealth and a more even distribution of economic power.

In practical terms the Second Plan postulated a development outlay of Rs 4,800 crores (£3,600 million), of which Rs 2,559 crores was to be expenditure incurred by the government of India and Rs 2,241 crores by the governments of the States. On this basis, plan expenditure would work out at something like the rather alarming average figure of Rs 950 crores per annum. Indeed, the financial chapter of the plan presented a set of figures calculated to chill the blood of any but the most courageous finance minister.

It is no derogation to the series of most able administrators who have held the Indian finance portfolio to say that it was only because it was politically underwritten by Pandit Nehru that the financial implications of the Second Plan were regarded as feasible, and therefore acceptable, by the country and the world. Of the Rs 4,800 crores of funds projected, the plan assumed that no less than one third should accrue by devices whose inflationary character was but thinly disguised. For example, deficit financing was put at Rs 1,200 crores and, when account had been taken of all other receipts which might be expected (including some receipts which a cautious accountant would probably prefer to classify as doubtful), there would be a gap of Rs 400 crores 'to be covered by additional measures to raise domestic resources'. Thus, under the most favourable circumstances, and if all went well, $33\frac{1}{3}$ per cent of a plan which—having regard to India's problems—cannot be said to have been overambitious, was to be conjured out of thin air or very nearly so. But in tackling a five year plan in this way India had accepted, rightly or wrongly, that its economic programme must henceforth reflect needs rather than resources. The financial purists were shocked, and there can be little doubt that the decision to proceed on these bold but unorthodox assumptions was made by Jawaharlal Nehru himself. No other minister carried enough political armament.

In return for the major burdens proposed by way of taxation, borrowing and a sizeable injection of deficit financing, Pandit Nehru was confident that the country would make a substantial stride forward in both agriculture and industry. It was estimated there would be an increase of 21 million acres under cultivation and $3\frac{1}{2}$ million acres of hitherto unused or unusable land were to be reclaimed. As a result of these and other measures, foodgrain production would rise by 15 per cent from 65 million tons in 1955–6 to 75 million tons in 1960–1, allowing daily consumption to be increased from 17·2 oz to 18·3 oz per adult, which by European standards would still be a pitifully meagre ration. Larger percentage increases were planned for non-edible crops. *Per capita* consumption of electricity was to double in the five years following 1955–6 to reach 50 units in 1960–1, by which time it was planned that every town with a population of 10,000 or more would be able to draw power from the various grids which criss-crossed the country. Ten million new non-agricultural employment opportunities were to be created in commerce and industry, the expansion of which was expected to proceed rapidly as public-sector production added to India's annual steel output another 2 million tons by the end of the Second Plan. The privately owned steel-works were also scheduled to raise output from 1·25 million tons to 2·3 million tons by 1958. Other basic industries, such as coal, heavy engineering and electrical equipment, fertilisers, chemicals, cement and the like, were given new and ample production targets. Such were a few of the highlights of the Second Plan. It was anticipated that, as a result of the effort which the plan called for in every department of the economy, the national income would have risen by 25 per cent by 1961.

But the plan ran into heavy weather almost from the start, and it was not long before it was in obvious difficulty. The first major obstacle to be encountered (plenty of others later showed themselves) was the running down of India's foreign exchange reserves at a much quicker rate than had been planned. While a government can make good a shortage of its own money by a deliberate act of currency creation, no such device is possible in respect to foreign currencies required for purchases abroad. A feature of the Second Plan was that it depended upon a much larger programme of imports of capital goods and equipment from abroad than anything which had gone before. During the First Plan, India's foreign exchange reserves had actually increased from Rs 723·07 crores at the end of the financial year 1951–2 to Rs 746·14 crores (say £560 million) in 1955–6. This was a respectable amount of 'till money' having regard to the volume of India's international trade and its balance-of-payments position at that time. But it did not provide a sufficient cushion to carry the heavy foreign exchange outgoings which were implicit in the Second Plan.

The written text of the plan contemplated a total foreign exchange deficit over the five years of Rs 1,100 crores (£825 million) which would be reduced by drawing down the reserves by Rs 200 crores during this period. The remaining gap of Rs 900 crores was to be filled '(a) by floating public issues in foreign money markets; (b) by arranging for bankers' credits and export credits for the supply of goods from foreign countries; (c) by borrowing from the International Bank for Reconstruction and Development and the newly formed International Finance Corporation; (d) by loans and grants from other international institutions such as the United Nations Technical Assistance Administration or the proposed Special United Nations Technical Fund for Economic Development; (e) through private foreign investment; and finally, (f) through loans and grants from friendly foreign governments'.[1] It will be necessary, said the authors of the Second Plan, 'for the country to take advantage of all these sources of finance for meeting the foreign exchange requirements of the plan'.

We can say straight away and without hesitation that Pandit Nehru had no great desire to float public issues in foreign money markets, which he regarded as part of the sinister machinery of international capitalism and therefore to be avoided. The City of London had traditionally been the place where India had made its external borrowings, but no new Indian issue had been floated there since the early 1930s when Indian loans were still guaranteed by the British government. Even if India had wished, it is doubtful whether, twenty years later, Indian loans—no longer enjoying trustee status— could have been placed on the London market.

Today the point is of no more than academic interest. By the end of the financial year 1956–7, the external reserves had fallen to Rs 526·83 crores. In one year of the Second Plan, India had lost more than the Rs 200 crores of foreign currency which was supposed to be the contribution of the reserves to the balance of payments deficit over the whole five year period. In each succeeding year there was a further precipitate drop until, by the end of March 1961, the reserves stood at Rs 136·25 crores (say £102 million)—less than a fifth of the amount they had been at the end of the First Plan. The strengths and weaknesses of a national economy are reflected in its balance of payments; apart from its immediate significance for India's short-term solvency, the swift decline in its reserves of foreign exchange illuminated, as nothing else could have done, the wide gulf between its industrialisation projects and the means of their fulfilment.

As soon as the reality of the situation became clear, the Indian authorities took vigorous, practical and, in some cases, unpleasant steps to staunch the out-flow of foreign exchange which reached flood proportions in 1957 and 1958. Severe cuts were made in imports, 500 items being taken off the open general license in one swoop; facilities for travel abroad were sharply curtailed; foreign expenditure generally came under closer scrutiny and was rationed. All the measures with which the post-war world has become familiar in many exchange crises were brought into play—all, that is, except a further devaluation of the rupee, which had been devalued along with the rest of the sterling group of currencies in 1949.

By such pinching and scraping India could possibly just break even on its current trading transactions, but it was by now abundantly clear that it could not hope by this means alone to finance the import of the many capital goods required to complete the Second and subsequent plans. If India was to carry through vital parts of the prepared plan, it was now quite certain that it needed the assurance of external aid on a scale considerably in excess of anything previously visualised. The money might not be immediately needed, but the plan could go forward smoothly only on the basis of assurances that when dollars or sterling or deutschmark or yen were needed they would be forthcoming. Thus, towards the end of 1956 the World Bank (already a substantial creditor) formed what has come to be known as the 'Aid India Consortium' through which all financial assistance to India from the western countries*— which in effect means most of India's external aid—is channelled after discussion between the donors and with India itself. Apart from the World Bank, which services the Consortium, the original members of the latter were the International Development Association (an affiliate of the World Bank), the United States, the United Kingdom, Canada, West Germany and Japan. Later, and at varying intervals, these parties were joined by France, Italy, Austria, Belgium and the Netherlands. The United States is the largest individual donor

---

* Though Australia and New Zealand, as Commonwealth countries, and certain uncommitted countries such as Norway and Switzerland have contributed to India's aid programme, the chief non-consortium donor is the USSR which has been giving assistance since 1955. India is both a recipient from and a donor to the Colombo Plan.

of aid and as a general principle stipulates that its annual appropriation shall not exceed the combined total of the amount subscribed by the other countries. Receiving assistance through this kind of international agency was a logical method of dealing with India's problem, and we may be sure was a more agreeable arrangement to its prime minister than the alternative of *ad hoc* borrowing.

Yet in spite of all the difficulties—financial, administrative, climatic, human and the rest—which were encountered, the Second Five Year Plan accomplished a great deal of what it set out to do. Original calculations may have been made upon assumptions which were altogether too slick and complacent, but in the light of Britain's own recent record, for all that it is an experienced engineering nation, of highly expensive failures or delays in the field of nuclear missiles, Englishmen at least cannot afford to be too critical of the rather wild arithmetic of India's plan. Planning in the 'developing' world is somewhat like the modern aircraft industry: something which is new and bigger and inevitably more expensive is always emerging to make last year's model completely out of date. Nothing is ever set for very long; the obsolescence rate, especially for ideas, is high; new objectives and fresh horizons are always coming into the planners' vision.

With the end of the Second Plan in 1961, India had behind it a decade of planning experience. It was time to take stock of the results, and the opening pages of the Third Plan Outline attempt to draw up a balance sheet of the credits and debits which must be set to the account of ten years of planning. During the First Plan national income had increased by 18 per cent as against a target of 12 per cent; on the other hand in the Second Plan period the increase had been 20 per cent against a target of 25 per cent. But the net gain was less than the figures suggested. In the ten years between 1951 and 1961, the population had risen by 77 million from 361 million to 438 million. India was rather like a man running up a descending escalator—just about able to hold his own. It was calculated that, at 1960–1 prices, average annual per capita income had advanced by Rs 46, from Rs 284 to Rs 330, which is not much more than £25 ($70) per head—say ten shillings ($1·50) a week.

However, interesting as these statistical abstractions may be, they were not as convincing as the physical evidence of progress which was to be found on the ground and in the soil of India itself. Agricultural progress is subject to more or less exact measurement. We find that the output of foodgrains rose by over 20 million tons to 76 million tons in 1961, in which year the index of agricultural production (1949 = 100), which embraces both food and cash crops, stood at 135: a gain of 41 per cent since 1951. The record in industrial production was even more spectacular. Between 1951 and 1961, the index advanced by 94 per cent. By the end of the Second Plan, the three new state-owned steelworks had started production, and the output of steel ingots had increased from 1·4 million tons in 1950–1 to 3·5 million tons in 1960–1, and that of pig iron from 350,000 tons to 900,000 tons. Work on the three public-sector steelworks—built with British, Russian and West German collaboration at Durgapur, Bhilai and Rourkela— was largely concentrated into the Second Plan period. To have got three large new steelworks going more or less at one time would have been regarded as a considerable triumph in most countries, but taken in conjunction with the many other things which the Indian administration was trying to get under way simultaneously, was little short of a miracle. The two privately owned steelworks, which provided a useful source of know-how and experience, were also considerably expanded. Major production advances were made in a whole variety of industries, including aluminium, diesel engines, electric cables, fertilisers, automobiles, paper and paper-board and many other things. The way was being cleared for the establishment of those metal-using industries whose development was to be a feature of the Third Plan.

Early in 1960, at the invitation of the World Bank and the government of India, a mission of three internationally distinguished bankers—Sir Oliver (now Lord) Franks, Dr Herman J. Abs and Mr Alan Sproull—visited India and reported their general impressions about the problems of development in that country. The mission studied the situation when the Second Five Year Plan was well into its second half and when the Third Plan was already beginning to take shape in the minds of the authorities. The bankers' findings were of a

general character, but their validity has been fully confirmed
in the intervening five years. Like everyone else who knows the
country, they were impressed by the high quality of many of
its politicians, administrators and businessmen. But they also
noted that managerial talent was scarce: a proposition to which
Indians themselves do not always readily assent. They also
remarked that India's experience of planning since 1951 had
inevitably involved a number of miscalculations, but that it
seemed much had been learnt from these about the techniques
of planning and of control. They advocated a re-examination of
marginal projects. (Such an examination had in fact been
taking place since the onset of the foreign exchange crisis.)
By marginal projects the mission meant those for which the
need was least obvious; and on this sort of question there is
always bound to be a conflict of views. The three bankers
thought that, comparatively speaking, the agricultural sector
of the economy came off second best, and considered it highly
desirable that it should receive in the remainder of the Second
Plan, and in the allocation of resources for the Third, a share
of investment commensurate with its importance. 'The problem of educating 50 million farmers in improved techniques
must clearly be approached on a selective basis rather than
thinly dispersed over the entire agricultural front.' Most
important, perhaps, the mission drew attention to the simple
fact that the greater the pressure for industralisation, the
greater the need for imports—for the time being at least. This
had not always been clearly acknowledged, even in the highest
quarters, where it was somewhat naively assumed that each
addition to industrial capacity represented a saving in imports.
'The emphasis given in the programs of industrial development
to import saving by no means implies, however, that the import
requirements of India will necessarily follow a declining trend
for the next 5, 10 or 15 years.'

Lord Franks and his colleagues advocated a closer look at
India's low money rates which created the illusion that capital
was not actually a scarce resource. They also had some wise
things to say about public as against private enterprise which,
as a subject of debate, was attracting much attention at that
time. They noted *inter alia* that India was one of the cheapest
steel producers in the world. Looking to the future, they

envisaged that outside assistance on a substantial scale would be necessary for a long period of time if India was to carry its plans through to completion. If the assistance required were made available entirely in the form of long- or short-term loans on normal commercial terms, the resulting debt-service burden would almost certainly impose an intolerable strain on the balance of payments in the future. Over the long term, aid on liberal terms with tolerable repayment terms would have to take the form of government-to-government assistance. This has been done by the development and extension of the consortium idea, which co-ordinates the aid of an increasing number of countries. Multilateralism provides the best way of getting the greatest benefit from a given volume of aid. The mission stressed that foreign assistance created problems for both the donor and receiver countries. It also urged the great importance of a realistic food programme in the face of the almost certain risk of crop failures from time to time. Already the practical helpfulness of the American 'Public Law 480'* was becoming evident, and the present writer is amongst those who hold the view that without this particular piece of legislation much of Indian and other 'planning' would have run to waste. Taken as a whole, the Franks Mission report provided a valuable, though not uncritical, imprimatur to the Five Year Plans as far as they had then gone.

When Pandit Nehru died in 1964, the Third Plan had just run the third year of its course. During this period many things had happened to remind India that the best laid and most carefully prepared of schemes often go astray. The quality of India's leadership had been faltering, and Nehru had for some time

---

* Public Law 480 is an American legislative device, whereby the US Congress authorises the sale of surplus commodities (mostly foodstuffs) to developing countries against payment in local currency. For the developing countries this conserves scarce foreign exchange; at the same time it enables the US to make wise use of its agricultural surpluses. The local currencies (or counter-part funds as they are commonly known) which accrue are spent by the US administration on objects, or invested by them in projects, in the territories concerned which are mutually agreed with the government of the developing country. Just as Lend-Lease was intended to meet the conditions of the war, so P.L. 480 is designed to help the developing countries in their special difficulties.

been visibly a sick and ailing man. A humiliating defeat had been inflicted by the Chinese on India's armed forces in the Himalayan areas of Ladakh and the North East Frontier. Relations with Pakistan (which had launched a fresh diplomatic offensive over Kashmir) were worse than they had been for some time, and poor monsoon rains had seriously affected agricultural production. Amid this sea of troubles, Third Plan targets seemed of small account. Some Indians were inclined to argue that one of China's chief objectives was to disrupt the Third Plan, which it disliked because it represented a demo-cratic alternative to its own totalitarian methods. China may well have not particularly wished the plan to succeed, but there is no evidence that the invasion of India was anything other than a diplomatic and military move in the frontier dispute. Some measure of the extent to which performance was falling behind the prescribed timetable may be gleaned from the fact that, during the first three years of the Third Plan, there had been a rise of 9·5 per cent in national income giving an annual increase of about 3.1 per cent against a target of more than 5 per cent per annum. But in a country like India, national income statistics—which are in any case a somewhat esoteric study—are perhaps not always a true indication of progress.

A more reliable guide is the price and availability of food-grains. Here the situation by mid-1965 was scarcely indicative of a nation marching confidently towards the goal of plenty. In many parts of the country, prices of food crops had risen to unprecedented heights. The basic cause of what had, by then, developed into a critical situation was not profiteering or maldistribution (though these were contributories) but a real and acute shortage of cereals: in other words a failure to raise agricultural output sufficiently. The Third Plan output target for foodgrains to be attained by 1965–6 was 100 million tons per annum, consisting of 45 million tons of rice, 15 million tons of wheat, 23 million tons of other cereals and 17 million tons of pulses. The 1963 crop was 77½ million tons, or 23 per cent below the target set for 1966—the final year of the Third Plan.

Urban areas in northern India, and in Calcutta especially, were the places most affected by the periods of near-famine in 1964 and 1965. There was continuous disagreement between the government and public opinion about its causes. The authorities stuck obstinately to the view that hoarding, unscrupulous trading and speculation, backed by 'black or unaccounted' money, were the main reasons for the shortage. Their critics maintained that agricultural production had failed to keep pace with the rapid increase in population, rising incomes, a generally higher standard of living and the greater ability of the farmer to control or withold supplies for urban markets. Furthermore, they alleged that the government's zonal distribution policies, by impeding the free movement of foodgrains, had aggravated the shortages in deficit states. There was a good deal of truth in what both sides said; but what was clear and indisputable was that, up to the half way mark of the Third Plan, agricultural policy had failed to break through the vicious circle of food shortages with which the Indian economy has been regularly afflicted since independence. So serious was the situation at one time that wheat shipments from Australia to the United Kingdom were diverted to Indian ports and fresh supplies of grain under 'Public Law 480' were negotiated with the United States.

In the industrial sector, the mid-term record of the Third Plan was somewhat better, though here again the original plan targets will not be reached by 1966. Over the five-year period it was confidently expected that industrial output would increase by 70 per cent, or at the average rate of 11 per cent each year. The first year of the plan produced a rise in output of 6.5 per cent per annum and the second a slightly better rate of 8 per cent. However, it seems most unlikely that the 70 per cent cumulative increase will be attained by 1966. The National Council for Applied Economic Research at New Delhi, in a survey of the Indian economy as at November 1963, gave as the main causes of the lag in industrial growth during the first two years of the plan acute shortages of four key requisites: coal, foreign exchange, power and transport. The foreign exchange shortage was the most difficult because it was the deficiency India could do least to remedy. The other shortages have become progressively less important as various bottlenecks have been cleared up: for instance, the railways now claim to have more capacity than traffic offerings. Industrial development in the Third Plan has had as its central objective the attainment by

India of self-sustaining growth as quickly as possible, and within this formula industrial priorities have been so arranged as to try to make the country progressively independent of imports. Policy has had the dual purpose of promoting the growth of such industries as would reduce the country's import bill, and of encouraging those other industries with export prospects and potentialities. For the time being the former is the more important of the two aims.

Results have been uneven. Investment in industries designed to save imports has usually achieved its objectives and reduced foreign expenditure on a particular article or component, but such investment has not yet made possible any reduction in the overall level of imports. Nonetheless, it cannot be said that, because of this, the large investment in industry has not been worthwhile. India has made a quite deliberate choice in favour of creating large-scale, mostly capital-intensive, industries such as iron and steel, heavy engineering, chemicals, oil production and refining and basic chemicals. These are the foundations on which the country intends to build the rest of its industrial structure, though the wisdom of the decision to create a heavy industrial base has been much debated inside and outside India. But the fact is that the possible courses of action were restricted by circumstances. India's considerable resources in iron ore and coal clearly decreed that, if it was going to industrialise at all, the start should be with iron and steel. Had India ignored the natural advantages it possesses in these, none of its economic planning would have made sense. Three new steelworks in the Second and Third Plans may sound a lot, but they are no more than India needs. Indeed, a plausible case can be made out for the fourth and even the fifth public-sector steelworks now under consideration.

4

THE MIDDLE WAY

Nehru, who apparently had enjoyed abundant good
health for most of his life, might reasonably have expected to see
the completion of the Third Plan before he handed over the
reins of government, or death claimed him in that last embrace
which Mahatma Gandhi once described as being 'of the incomparable friend'. In fact, in chronological terms he only
lived to see the working out of the first two, and a half of the
third, of his country's Five Year Plans. The question arises (or
will arise for future historians and commentators): where did
Jawaharlal Nehru stand in all this? In what direction was his
influence exercised? How powerful was he at the centre of the
planning process, and was his personality just as effective on the
periphery? Did he rely too much or too little on his own
judgement? If the latter, who were his chief mentors? A stream
of such questions come to mind. We must try to answer some of
them, for a measure of information on these points is greatly
important to a proper understanding of the years during which
Nehru exercised almost undisputed power.

There is a tendency to relate Nehru's economic opinions to
recorded Congress Party resolutions in the same field, and to
equate the growth of his socialism with the leftward drift of
Congress official pronouncements. This is much too ingenuous to
serve as an explanation of his complicated thought processes.
In any case, as a theory it does not square with the facts. In a
stimulating essay, "Heralding a New Epoch", in a symposium
entitled *A Study of Nehru*,[1] published to celebrate Panditji's
seventieth birthday, Professor P.C. Mahalanobis, FRS, founder
of the Indian Statistical Institute, describes the evolution of
Nehru as a planner as distinct from Nehru the socialist.

c

Professor Mahalanobis, related to the gifted Tagore clan and a distinguished mathematician and physicist, is the father of modern statistical practice in India and was the first person to introduce something like accurate crop forecasting by scientific sampling methods. For good or ill, Mahalanobis had considerable personal influence with the prime minister in regard to planning. There were periods when he was in high favour; there were others when he was not. But when his star was in the ascendant, Mahalanobis had the close attention of Pandit Nehru in the special context of planning, and some people affect to regard the professor as a sort of *éminence grise* operating in the wings of the planning machine. Be that as it may, Mahalanobis was in a unique position to observe the various stages by which Nehru's planning philosophy took shape, for with the passage of time he became virtually the prime minister's personal economic adviser and sowed the seeds of many of the techniques which were subsequently adopted.

Nehru and Professor Mahalanobis had known each other socially for a number of years; their meetings had chiefly taken place under the roof of the poet Rabindranath Tagore. But it was not until 1940—or two years after the Congress Party's National Planning Committee had been set up—that they first talked about economic planning for India: a discussion which, Mahalanobis recalls, began at the dinner table and did not end until the clock had struck two the following morning. In fact, it was a dialogue which was to continue, with occasional intermissions, for practically the next quarter of a century. Mahalanobis was primarily a statistician and only incidentally an economist; the professor's importance to Nehru was that he had at last found someone with the necessary scientific skill to organise and quantify his economic theories and with whom he could freely discuss them—which he continued to do without disloyalty either to his ministers or to the Planning Commission. Over the years Mahalanobis became a sort of private and unofficial keeper of the prime minister's economic conscience: a role for which there is no lack of precedents to be found nearer home.*

Professor Mahalanobis advances an interesting theory about Nehru's approach to planning, and one which I (with at least

* His official title was 'Honorary Statistical Adviser to the Prime Minister'.

a journalist's acquaintance with the late prime minister's mind)
find entirely plausible. Mahalanobis divides planning into two
categories: the first he calls the 'concentrated' sector, in which
decisions can be made and implemented by a small group of
persons, and the other he terms the 'diffused' sector, in which
decision and implementation depend on the concurrence and
participation of a very large number, maybe hundreds of
millions of persons. A 'concentrated' example would be
decisions regarding the establishment of a steel plant; a
'diffused' example would be the carrying through of a large
family-planning programme or a nationwide scheme of
compulsory savings, which would require organisation and
explanation over a vast area at the grass roots level. In spite of
Nehru's gift of being able to speak to the masses in language
which they understood, and despite his hold over them in many
other respects and his ability to mobilise them for political
ideas (*e.g.* in support of the Freedom Movement), Mahalanobis
gives it as his opinion that, so far as planning was concerned,
Nehru was 'generally more effective in decisions in the
concentrated sector, for example, in regard to industrialisation'.
But Nehru contended that a big and variegated country like
India would not hold together without what he himself called
'emotional integration'. Hence, although he so often spoke in
vague terms about such abstractions as institutional changes,
social upheaval, agrarian revolutions and the like, he was in
reality at his best in planning and making decisions of a
'concentrated' character. This is a curious and I believe
hitherto unrevealed dichotomy in Nehru's personality. It is
borne out by the present deputy-chairman of the Planning
Commission, Asoka Mehta, who says of Nehru 'always his
main contribution was the *élan* he imparted, rarely organisational consolidation'.

Dr V. K. R. V. Rao, vice-chancellor of Delhi University and
one who has been close to the centre of affairs for many years,
says in his contribution to *A Study of Nehru* that Nehru could not
be regarded as a socialist in the accepted sense of the term.
His concern for the masses, both urban and rural, was humanitarian in kind and this invevitably meant he was in favour of
reducing inequalities as between individuals and of a programme of planned economic development for the nation. His

was, in fact, the only policy for a country of chronic poverty, the extent of which was increasing every day. Dr Rao quotes the Indian leader as saying on one occasion: 'It is not a question of the theory of communism, or socialism or capitalism. It is a question of hard fact. In India, if we do not ultimately solve the basic problems of our country—the problems of food, clothing, housing and so on—it will not matter whether we call ourselves capitalists, socialists, communists or anything else . . . our method need not necessarily be an extreme method belonging to rival ideologies; it may be something in between.' This was one of the several notable occasions on which Nehru revealed himself as a man of the middle way.

But the performance of a political leader who chooses a middle course is bound, for one reason or another, to cause dissatisfaction among important elements which are more definitely lined up on the left or right hand sides of the road. Inevitably Nehru's planning and other policies for occupying the 'commanding heights' of the Indian economy failed to satisfy those of his countrymen who professed to be and called themselves socialists. At the same time, such policies were radical enough to seem threatening and vexatious to those holding opposite views: organised commerce and industry, the shareholder and rentier classes, and the not inconsiderable conservative elements in the Indian middle class. It was in many ways Nehru's supreme achievement that he managed both to convince reformers that society was being reorganised and the economy being made to move in a direction favourable to India's mute millions, and also to reconcile the more cautious elements to the process of change and reassure them that in the mixed economy of the future there would be a valued place for the talents, individual initiative, thrift and other qualities which have always marked the upper-middle grades of Indian society. There was no intellectual sleight-of-hand in this. Nehru's 'socialist pattern' of society was very definitely not intended to be a classless society from which all differences would be smelted out in the fierce crucible of revolution.

Though the Five Year Plans represented the high point of Nehru's socialist theories and thinking, there were many other ways by which he sought to reshape the economy. Reforming land tenure, co-operative farming, state trading, the regulation of private enterprise in commerce and industry—these were the directions along which his enquiring mind was constantly moving. The result was the passage through parliament of an impressive total of fairly drastic legislation.

The origins of India's system of land tenure went back many centuries before the emergence of the East India Company as a dominant force in Indian economic and political life. There was an astonishing variety of forms of tenure in different parts of the country, but three broad categories of ownership were distinguishable: Zamindari, Mahalwari and Ryotwari. The immensely complicated structure of the Indian system of land tenure is almost unintelligible to the uninstructed western reader and need not detain us here. Someday, sooner or later, an Indian government would manifestly be obliged to overhaul and simplify the entire system, which in most parts of the country resulted in the fragmentation of the land into un-economic units.

Land ownership, land taxation and new and better methods of farming have always been political dynamite. Moreover, in newly independent India the 'land question' was partly the concern of the central government and partly the responsibility of the States: a circumstance which did not make reform any easier. The complicated picture is well described by H. Vankatasubbia who says that 'in the post-independence period there was a large middle ground in the land economy of the country between the landless wage labourers at the one end and the labourless landowners at the other. This ground was taken up by those who possessed land, whether or not they were the owners of it, or in addition had established proprietorship over it in some degree between outright ownership at one end and pure tenancy-at-will at the other.'[2] This describes the whole fantastic spectrum of land tenancy. A feature of the system was the existence of an army of intermediaries who stood between the cultivator and the government. The dubious practice of farming land revenues through this chain of intermediaries had never been fully abolished. In fact, in some places there was more farming of tax revenue than there was of the land. This was the position at the time of independence.

Such a state of affairs was a drag on the economy and a

grievous offence in the eyes of an administration pledged to a socialist pattern of society. The First Five Year Plan recognised the significance of land ownership and cultivation to the whole process of economic development. The Second Plan carried the process a stage further, and the Third Plan had as one of its principal agencies the Panel on Land Reform. This worked through four committees to deal with problems relating to tenancy reform, ceilings on holdings, settlement of landless agricultural workers and the consolidation of holdings. Intermediary interests have been acquired over a wide area and considerable headway has been made with the whole programme of reform. But, as matters relating to agriculture and the land fall within the jurisdiction of the States' administrations, progress has been uneven. West Bengal, for example, has acquired all rent-receiving interests, but at mid-1963 there were still a few intermediaries to be legislated for in Assam, Gujarat, Madras and Maharashtra. Several hundred crores of rupees had been paid out in cash or in bonds as compensation for rights acquired by the government. With these few exceptions the Third Plan Outline estimated that by 1961 the abolition of intermediary tenures represented by zamindaries, jagirs and inams had been completed, that more than 20 million tenants had been brought into direct relationship with the government, and that considerable areas of waste and private forest land had come under the management of the authorities.

The purposes of land reform, as officially proclaimed, were firstly to remove such impediments to increased agricultural production as arise from the agrarian structure of the past; and secondly to eliminate from the system elements of exploitation and social injustice. We may first consider the latter point. A dozen or so years ago, the level of rents commonly paid by tenants-at-will, non-occupancy tenants and sharecroppers over the greater part of India was one half of the produce and sometimes more.* There were other incidentals, too, which added to the ryot's total outgoings. All that has now been changed: in every State rents have been substantially reduced. For instance, in Gujerat, Maharashtra and Rajasthan the maximum rent now

* Many agricultural rents in India are still levied in kind, though the Planning Commission strongly urges commutation of rents in kind into cash payments wherever possible.

stands at one-sixth of the produce; in Assam and Kerala the rent payable is about one-fourth of the produce or less. Furthermore, security of tenure has been established and, for better or for worse, legislation providing for a ceiling on land holdings has been enacted in all the States except the Punjab. Whether this limitation is a good or a bad thing remains to be seen; it cannot be more harmful to Indian agriculture than the previous practice of unlimited fragmentation.

But to return to the first of our propositions, which was that a less archaic system of land tenure—one from which in fact all private gain had been removed and the state become a kindly and beneficent landlord—would result in increased agricultural production. Has it in fact produced better cultivation and bigger crops? This is one of those large omnibus questions to which no single or exact answer is possible. Agricultural production as a whole has increased in the last ten years, but just how much of the additional productivity is due to an improved system of land tenure it is impossible to say; the use of improved methods of cultivation has without question been the major factor in improved output. For instance, Russian, British, American and Czech tractors are now to be seen at work all over the Punjab, and they, and the increased use of fertilisers and irrigation, have undoubtedly made the Punjabi farmers, the finest in Asia, even more successful than in the past. In some other parts of India, tractors—the great symbol of development—have not been so successful. Land reform may not have done all that was once expected of it, and it is not possible to measure with any exactitude its direct effect upon agricultural production, but without doubt it has been a major step in the right direction and has made progress in the rural areas possible also in a number of other ways.

Over the years Nehru personally did much to arouse the enthusiasm of the peasant and cultivator not only for a more equitable system of land tenure but also for better methods of production and distribution. Even so, he was compelled to recognise that the Indian farmer's innate conservatism sets a limit to the pace at which it is possible to carry through reform. At one time Nehru was much attracted to the idea of collective farming, and indeed he put forward proposals for its adoption in certain areas. The opposition to these was, however, so

spontaneous and violent that he made a swift tactical retreat
and the matter was not raised again. The Third Five Year Plan
gingerly discusses co-operative farming (something quite
different from collective farming), which it describes as 'a
voluntary movement' in which 'there should be no question
of compelling any cultivator to join'. As well as being conservative, the Indian farmer is also highly individualistic. Thus, the
agrarian revolution over which Nehru presided was to a large
extend a 'revolution by consent'. With the absorption of the
former Princely States and the extinction of the old landlord
rights, rural India was brought abruptly into the modern age
in so far as legislation could achieve such a metamorphosis. In
less than a decade, the landed gentry—who from the time of the
Moghuls had been the most durable element in Indian society
—lost their position as feudal potentates. The wiser among them
had already begun to look for careers in business or the administrative and military services, or even in States' politics.

Socialist dogma apart, Nehru had to support the undoubtedly
valid argument that nothing short of nationalisation would
suffice to deal with the immensely complex and politically
inflammable land question. But the same could not be said about
other nationalisation measures. The Bank of England, the
oldest and most important central banking institution in the
Commonwealth, had been nationalised in 1946 on the grounds
that the post-war Labour government in Britain should be
able to bring its ownership, and with it control of the country's
credit and banking mechanism, under the direct surveillance
of the government. What was the proper thing for the oldest of
central banks was obviously the right thing for one of the
newest, the Reserve Bank of India inaugurated by the British-
India administration in 1935. Such was the thinking of the
first government of independent India which certainly had the
more compelling argument that, as the country had now severed
its political ties with Britain, the rupee had acquired a new
monetary status whose sovereignty could only be properly
expressed through a state-owned central banking institution.
This would defend the value of the currency, advise the government of the day, carry out the duties of registrar of the public
debt, supervise the new and as yet ill-organised gilt-edged

market and perform the traditional role of lender of last resort to a rather undisciplined money market. There were the inevitable grave warnings in parliament and the press that nationalisation of the Reserve Bank was the first step down the slippery slope to economic perdition, but no one who has seen the bank in operation and taken account of events since independence can have the slightest doubt that its acquisition by government was a wise—indeed the only—decision in all the circumstances.

How much of this was at the direct instance of Nehru is difficult to assess. It was certainly the sort of thing which could count on his warm approval, and he was the head of the administration by which it was enacted. To that extent a large part of the credit must go to him. The governor of the bank who carried through the nationalisation, Shri C. D. Deshmukh, has recorded that the board of the bank sincerely believed the government's decision to be unnecessary, but undertook to co-operate with the authorities to the fullest extent.[3] National-lisation of the Reserve Bank was effected on January 1, 1949, and was the first major operation of this kind by the new government. Six years later, in 1955, the government acquired a major shareholding in the Imperial Bank of India, with which the government of India and the Reserve Bank had always had the closest relations. It was renamed the State Bank of India.

In the collection of lectures just referred to, Chintaman Deshmukh comments on the credit structure for both agriculture and industry, and in this context says that a lacuna still persisted which 'could not be rectified by Government, so long as it had no control over insurance companies and their investment policies'.[4] It was by no stray chance, therefore, that the government decided to nationalise all life companies and agencies and to consolidate their business into a single state-owned Life Insurance Corporation of India on September 4, 1956. This was perhaps the most comprehensive act of nationalisation that Nehru's government had yet undertaken. It is most unlikely that he had anything much to do with the details, but there can be no doubt that the principle had his unqualified blessing. The corporation is the biggest investor in the country today and has a tremendous influence on the stock and share markets of Calcutta and Bombay. As on December 31, 1961, its total investments amounted to approximately Rs 582 crores (£436½ million). It transacts foreign business in Aden, Fiji, Hongkong, Kenya, Malaya, Mauritius, Singapore, Tanganyika and Zanzibar, Uganda, and the United Kingdom: in fact, everywhere that British and Indian enterprise has established itself. One may question whether this was socialism in Nehru's sense of the word. But though it may not be socialism of the text-book variety, it was certainly a very practical step towards the promised establishment of a 'socialist pattern of society'.

Two other nationalisation enactments of less social import were the acquisition by the state in 1953 of all civil airlines. At the end of the war and in the early post-war years, there were one or two privately owned airlines in India which were extremely well-run; there were also a number of others with ageing second-hand aircraft and no capital reserves for their replacement. The government wisely decided to take over the whole industry, and has developed a network of airlines which serves the entire country and is of special use to the business community—who incidentally were originally loudest in their criticism of the administration's proposals. By the same enactment, it acquired an international air service, which by any standards is a credit to India and its original sponsors, Tatas. The remaining nationalisation act of importance was that by which the Kolar Gold Fields companies passed into the public sector. An important point of policy was involved in this operation, which was initiated by the government of the State of Mysore. The latter had doubtful authority for its action under the government of India's Industrial Policy Resolution of 1956, but in any case a sale by the company to the local government was a somewhat dubious proposition in view of the Mysore government's inability to raise the necessary cash. Eventually, the central government (which was the mining companies' principal customer) stepped in; a settlement which was satisfactory to both parties was negotiated, the British shareholders were paid out and the properties passed into the ownership and control of the government of India.

Of none of these measures can it be said they were motivated by a full blooded Marxism. There were said to be right wing and left wing factions in the Indian cabinet at the time; if so all the evidence would seem to indicate that Nehru preserved a strict balance between the two and did it with great skill. One has, of course, to remember that, with the possible exception of the nationalisation of life insurance, no single one of these acts touched the life of the people of India below the level of the upper middle classes. The Indian people were well accustomed to their government's performing tasks which in some other countries were regarded as commercial in origin, and as a result Nehru's first batch of nationalisation measures were far from revolutionary in their consequences. The banking system did its work under the leadership of the state-owned Reserve Bank much as it had done it under a Reserve Bank owned by shareholders. Apart from a number of first-class life insurance companies, there were many whose solvency might be questioned, and whose funds had been invested by their promoters in industries in which they had a risky personal stake. Thus some thousands of small policy holders were given a new sense of security; satisfactory arrangements were made for foreign insurers to wind up their business in the country and for the servicing of their outstanding policies to maturity. None of these things brought about earth-shaking changes in the Indian economy.

In the late 1950s there developed a great public debate on the relative merits of state versus private enterprise as a system of business and industrial organisation. The debate was largely of Nehru's own making for he threw down the gauntlet, as it were, on behalf of state enterprise at a widely publicised All-India Congress Committee seminar in Ootacamund at the end of the 1950s. Later, on several occasions, when addressing bodies of Indian businessmen or industrialists, he went out of his way to emphasise that there was no inherent conflict between the public and private sectors in India. Nonetheless, it seemed to many industrialists that, in an economy whose chief feature was its shortages, the scales were clearly weighted in favour of the public sector. Throughout much of the Nehru period there was really no effective parliamentary mouthpiece to speak on behalf of organised Indian business, which contains large, responsible and public spirited elements whose merits have

tended to be obscured by the misdemeanours of a few—
misdemeanours which have been eagerly seized upon by a
legislature only too ready to find fault with the private enterprise system. It would be stretching the facts to say that, even
now, there is a party which speaks effectively in parliament for
organised business and for the private sector. But in August
1959 there came into being a new political party called the
Swatantra (or Freedom) Party which claimed to be non-
communal in character and which is certainly conservative in
its outlook. The Swatantra Party was the first serious attempt
to organise a parliamentary opposition of the right to replace
the congeries of groups and independents who very occasionally
acted together in the lobbies.

As might be expected, a party composed of representatives
of big business, a dispossessed squirearchy and other stray
conservative elements, which the high tide of independence
had left in a stranded and exposed position in Indian life,
was regarded by Nehru as something of a political freak—
especially as it was anti-socialist, proclaiming in the forefront
of its initial statements of aims and objects: 'We are of the
opinion that social justice and welfare can be reached more
certainly and properly in other ways than through techniques
of so-called socialism . . . ' A good deal in a similar vein
followed. Nehru was frankly scornful; but though somewhat of
a mixed crew, the sponsors of the Swatantra Party contained
men of considerably above average ability and some who had
been prominent in the Congress Party. First and foremost was
C. R. Rajagopalachari, in his eighties but possessed of a rare
intellectual vigour. He has for many years been a truly vener-
able figure in Indian public life; a friend of Gandhi's, a former
chief minister of Madras and the first and last Indian governor-
general of the Dominion of India. But for the fact that he is a
South Indian who does not speak Hindi, he might well have
been the first president of the independent republic of India.
'Rajaji' brought enormous influence and prestige to the new
party at its birth. Of a different *genre* were Sir Homi Mody,
M. R. Masani and K. M. Munshi—the first two having been
closely associated with the House of Tata, Bombay's leading
business group, while Munshi had been a former home minister
of Bombay and had done a term as governor of Uttar Pradesh.

But perhaps the strangest member of this unusual band of founding fathers of the new party was Professor N. G. Ranga, who for the whole of his political life had been associated with the peasant movement and agrarian reform in various parts of India. Amongst other things, Ranga is the author of *Panchayat Landlordism versus Peasant Economy*—hardly the sort of philosophy one would expect to find in a predominantly right-wing party. Yet it must be said in favour of Swatantra that, in contrast to some other opponents of the present government, it refrains from basing its case on communal or religious claims, and stands firmly for the rule of law and the authority of parliament.

At the last general election, held in 1962, the Swatantra Party won 18 seats in the Lok Sabha (lower house) and thus became the second largest opposition party, the Communist Party being the largest with 29 seats, and therefore the official opposition. Since then, however, the Communist Party of India, like Communists elsewhere, have lined up in two ideological camps and this division has been carried into the Indian parliament where the Communists are split into pro-Russian and pro-Chinese factions. The effect has been to make the Swatantra Party now the official opposition in the Lok Sabha. In the first fifty bye-elections held after the general election (i.e. up to the late summer of 1963) for the Union parliament and the State assemblies, it scored two or three victories, but most observers are agreed that it will take more than a handful of electoral gains for the Swatantra Party to offer a serious alternative to the Congress governments either at the centre or in the States.

The relatively weak position of organised trade and industry vis-à-vis the post-independence Congress Party (and therefore in relation to the government itself) is to some extent compensated by the agencies which have been established for the purpose of consulting business opinion. Apart from the Planning Commission and the attached National Development Council, which in their own spheres are engaged in a continuous dialogue with public opinion, over the years the government has set up a number of consultative bodies in which business interests have a place. The advice of their delegates may not always be taken, but at least they have an opportunity of expressing their views on matters which affect them closely. Examples of such consultative organisation are the Export-Import Council, the Control of Capital Issues Committee, the Central Advisory Council of Industries, etc. But these are not policy-making bodies so much as policy-reviewing agencies, and parliament is apt to regard itself as a police force supervising the private sector rather than a place where the latter's case should be listened to with some patience and understanding.

There have been one or two outstandingly able spokesmen for the private sector in the Lok Sabha from time to time, but in general the Congress back benches have been ill-informed about, and curiously indifferent to, the aims and achievements of privately owned Indian industry and business as a whole. As a result, some of the commercial legislation initiated and passed during the Nehru years has been more severe than wise. But the debate (now quiescent) on the respective merits of state and private enterprise was largely unreal; India requires them both and is seeking to evolve a system which gives ample opportunity for each to be developed.* Though Nehru had a strong personal preference for state ownership and management, it is to his credit that he sought to give the private sector as fair a deal as was possible in the political circumstances of his premiership. His greatest defect was to oversimplify economic propositions and to become impatient if his point of view was not quickly understood and accepted. He determined that the private sector should pay for the privilege of existing in a state dedicated to pursuit of the 'socialist pattern of society' and, presumably with his active encouragement, the high taxation and restrictive company legislation of recent years have been part of the price.

Nonetheless he genuinely sought to steer a middle course in economic affairs, and as long as he was at the helm it was unlikely that any kind of extreme action would be taken against the rentier class or privately owned trade and industry. Indeed, he was much too sensible to suppose that at this stage of its development India could get on without a substantial

* Though I agree with the statement that 'the country entering currently on nationhood is faced, at least in principle, with the interesting problem of selecting an economic system'. John Kenneth Galbraith, *Economic Development*, Harvard University Press and Oxford University Press, 1964, p. 23.

contribution from this most important and experienced sector of the economy.

Where then do we place Nehru in the complicated mosaic of India's economic policy? He was, of course, at the head and front of the now sizeable hierarchy of Indian planners. He brought to the business of planning much of its initial drive and momentum; in many ways he was a man in a desperate hurry. At the same time he was a gradualist and a man of the middle way. His goals were very rarely fully defined, and purely economic factors were too often mixed-up with political considerations. But he had a very clear vision of the direction in which he desired Indian economic policy to proceed and an understanding of how to get the elephantine and apparently immovable Indian administration to set its course in the same direction. Though he often talked the ideological language of the Left, and his occasional monologues on economic theory could be extremely baffling to the listener, there was also a hard, practical streak in his make-up which often led him intuitively to put first things first. In a country in which energy flags and programmes of all kinds naturally tend to get behind schedule, it is no bad thing to have some one at the top who is impatient for results, even if at times he appears a little unreasonable. In a sense Nehru personally underwrote India's first three five year plans; he staked a good deal of his political reputation on their success, and though the second and third plans have met with many difficulties and have failed to realise some of their most vital targets, their achievements have been more than sufficient to outweigh their shortcomings. In large measure this is due to Nehru, who not only rallied his own people behind the idea of planned development but, by reason of his stature outside India, helped to mobilise international support and fired the imagination of the free world for aid schemes that would have been regarded as impossible a few years earlier. It is no accident that India has become both the model and the laboratory for the study of practically every branch of planning and development. This is an important item in the Nehru legacy to his countrymen.

In the summer of 1965, a brief provisional outline of the Fourth Plan was made public. The Plan is to cover the years

1966 to 1971. As at present contemplated, expenditure will be
of the order of Rs 21,000/23,000 crores, say between £15,750
million and £17,250 million. Shastri laid down that this
plan must adhere strictly to two main principles: agriculture
is to have priority number one, and inflationary financing
should be avoided altogether. It is impossible to say whether
the second of these conditions is feasible until the Plan is laid
out in some detail. Meanwhile, it may be noted that the
avoidance of deficit inflationary expenditure was the ostensible
reason for the supplementary budget presented to the Indian
Parliament in August 1965. For the rest the Fourth Five Year
Plan, as might be expected, will almost certainly continue in
the pattern set by Nehru fifteen years ago for planning in a
parliamentary democracy.

5

MAKING A FOREIGN
POLICY

IN NO DEPARTMENT of government will the disappearance
of Pandit Nehru be more noticeable than in that which controls
India's external relations. The foreign policy of his successors
will almost certainly be pitched in a distinctly lower key and
therefore less idealistic and more workaday. But some of Nehru's
guiding principles in foreign affairs will survive for a long time
to come, for the quite simple reason that they are based upon
the realities of the situation—one of which is that, in terms of
power politics, India's poverty and lack of massive armed
strength are only to be compensated by a posture of objective-
ness and genuine moral authority. Other factors, like history
and geography, cannot be ignored; both have played a major
part in the shaping of India's attitude towards the outside
world, but perhaps not quite so much as some scholars and
commentators think. For India began to handle its own
external affairs at the precise moment after the second world
war when the whole technique of the old diplomacy—based on
private negotiations between governments—gave place to
public declamation on the floor of the United Nations. This
gave a literate and highly articulate administration, such as
India possessed, a tremendous advantage despite the power-
political weakness of the country. Furthermore, Nehru was a
world statesman. He did not need to go to New York to make a
pronouncement on international affairs; the world's press
came to Delhi to hear him. His activity in the field of foreign
policy was considerable: some of it was good and enduring
and some of it now seems bad; certainly none of it was negligible.

But first we should look back at the position as it was at the time of independence.

Until 1947 India had virtually no foreign policy of its own; such external relations as it had were fashioned at Westminster and, as they mostly related to obscure principalities in the East, were chiefly the concern of a handful of specialists in Whitehall and Delhi. By tradition India was the centre from which Britain's eastern empire was developed and consolidated. It was from India that Burma was occupied, that concessions were obtained on the Chinese mainland and for which the opium wars were fought; and it was from India, and with the aid of Indian trade and labour, that the British East African territories were brought into the sphere of British influence at the beginning of the present century. During the long period of Britain's expansion overseas, India was an outpost, a forward base, a garrison from which the metropolitan power operated. As a result it acquired a quite splendid army. But one thing India had no opportunity of evolving was a foreign policy of its own. This was to have important consequences for India when political independence came in 1947.

Another important fact is that British India's Foreign and Political Department, which managed India's somewhat limited external affairs and the central government's relations with the Princely States like Hyderabad and Baroda, was a service with relatively few Indians in it. It was staffed jointly from the army and the civil services, but—unlike the administrative, railway, medical and other branches of the civil service, which had a high proportion of Indians in them—the Foreign and Political Service was in the main a British preserve. Hence, when independence came in 1947, there was only a handful of Indian executive officers with previous experience of work in diplomatic missions abroad or who had studied foreign policy in any detail.

In a sense, therefore, India's relations with its neighbours may be said to have started from scratch in 1947. Yet this is not wholly true; if the new Indian government did not inherit a foreign policy or a foreign service, it was the heir to some at least of the foreign policy problems which had preoccupied the former administration for generations. It was not long before the new independent government in Delhi discovered that external problems do not change overnight because one administration has been replaced by another. Furthermore, the Congress Party government of Nehru came into power at a moment when the world—and particularly its eastern hemisphere—was in turmoil following the second world war and when many of the former guarantees of stability had disappeared. The Pax Britannica, for instance, which for a hundred years had been a sure guarantee of law and order in various parts of the world had ceased to operate, and a new world order, based on the division of the nations between two rival ideological camps, was coming into being.

It will be convenient to separate India's external relations into three main sectors. The first sector embraces those relations which oblige it to have a view about, or to take some action concerning, the great global issues which affect all of us. Nehru's policies in foreign affairs were highly critical of formal alliances and groupings (though it is noticeable that in recent years a marked change has occurred in Indian attitudes in this regard), and strongly supported disarmament proposals and the peacekeeping efforts of the United Nations. The second sector concerns relations with contiguous areas in which India claims a special interest: the Indian Ocean and the states along the country's frontiers. Outstanding in this sector is India's concern over the understanding negotiated in 1964 between China and Pakistan. The third sector involves India's relations with the Afro-Asian nations. Here both history and geography induce India to lend a sympathetic and understanding ear to the demands of this group for a larger voice in world affairs.

Affecting the attitudes of Indians to problems in these three sectors is the idea they have, with some reason, of their country as a bridge between Asia and the West: a role that was undoubtedly given shape and reality by Pandit Nehru, himself essentially the product of two hemispheres.

In an address at Columbia University, New York, in October 1949, Nehru gave a concise definition of the objectives of India's foreign policy in the following terms:

> The pursuit of peace, not through alignment with any major power or group of powers, but through an independent

approach to each controversial or disputed issue; the liberation of subject peoples; the maintenance of freedom, both
national and individual; the elimination of racial discrimination; and the elimination of want, disease and ignorance
which afflict the greater part of the world's population.

The first part of this passage is really an affirmation of the oft-
criticised and much misunderstood policy of non-alignment
which, in Indian minds at least, is quite distinct from any
kind of neutralism, however nominal the difference may
appear to western students of international problems. India's
involvement in the wars of the twentieth century was the
result, not of specifically Indian policy, but of its position as a
member state of the British Empire. Independence having
at last been obtained, Nehru and the great bulk of his fellow
countrymen were determined to avoid entanglements by which
India might be led into some future and vastly more devasting
conflict. Though decked out in grandiloquent terms, non-
alignment was a polite way of saying to the world: 'India is not
available for membership of any military pacts or alliances,
and from that point of view may we please be left out of your
plans for military and political coalitions.' At any rate, as a
policy non-alignment had the support of all thinking Indians
and was not just a fad which Nehru foisted on the country. It
is one of his more permanent legacies to India.

But non-alignment is not an end in itself and Nehru soon
discovered it was necessary to give his foreign policy a more
positive content. He put forward the *Panch Shila*, or five
principles of peace, which were first enunciated in the early
part of 1954 as principal points in the treaty between India
and Communist China regarding Tibet, and shortly afterwards
repeated in a joint declaration by Pandit Nehru and Chou
En-lai. In view of what has happened since, the five principles
of peace are worth recapitulating. They are: (1) mutual
respect for territorial integrity and sovereignty; (2) non-
aggression; (3) non-interference in internal affairs; (4) equality
and mutual benefit; and (5) peaceful coexistence. While non-
alignment had the support of the majority of the Indian
intelligentsia and the comparatively small number of others
who think about foreign affairs, it is doubtful if the *Panch Shila*,

as an expression of policy and code of conduct in international affairs, were ever regarded very seriously by the great bulk of the Indian people. The hard-bitten and cynical world outside received the five principles as a sort of diplomatists' Sermon on the Mount and a set of beatitudes for ministers and senior officials concerned with foreign affairs. Critics were not wanting who pointed to a measure of inconsistency between the high moral tone of *Panch Shila* and certain of India's own dealings with its neighbours. The unreality of *Panch Shila* as the basis of a foreign policy became clear as dealings with China—which had been specially associated with Nehru's original declamation of the principles—began to worsen. We shall have occasion to look more closely at this later on.

Still, despite the apparent desire to stand aside from the tensions and conflicts of the post-war world, India has had a good record of participation in international bodies and international decisions. Nehru confirmed India's existing obligations and was not averse to adding to them, so long as they conformed to his principle of non-alignment. India was a foundation member of the United Nations. Under the former British-Indian administration, India had subscribed to the original Bretton Woods agreements which resulted in the creation of the International Monetary Fund and the International Bank for Reconstruction and Development. Independent India has become an important client of both these institutions. The Indian government played a leading part in bringing about, if not peace, at least a cease-fire in Korea and Indochina, and in this capacity its efforts revealed far more understanding of the hard facts of international life than the famous five principles.

But perhaps the most significant of all India's international commitments is its membership of the Commonwealth: a circumstance due almost entirely to the personal authority of Nehru. Of the many public tributes paid to 'Panditji' when he died, none was more touching than that of Lord Mountbatten, who stressed the spirit of forgiveness and the lack of bitterness in the great Indian leader who had spent not a few years in British jails. It was this quality of magnanimity (not always pronounced in politicians) which enabled Nehru to look at the question of whether India should remain in the Commonwealth

through clear and unprejudiced eyes. Other influences amongst
many were, I think, the scrupulous manner in which the British
government divested itself of all responsibility for Indian
affairs once the independence bargain was made; there were
no reservations and nothing was held back. Britain asked for
no special protection for its still substantial commercial
interests in the country. There was also the realisation amongst
Indians that India still had many ties with other countries of
the Commonwealth and especially with Britain.

Even so, a factor of which not sufficient account has been
taken was the quick understanding which had been established
between the minds of Mountbatten and Nehru, once the former
had been drafted into the business of winding up the British
administration in India. Many other factors were doubtless
weighed in the balance before the final decision was made, but
it is unlikely that they would have counted for much if India's
first high-level contacts with Britian at the time of independence
had not been between men who had an instinctive understanding of each other. The part India under Nehru has played
in Commonwealth affairs is discussed in Chapter 8.

In one way, Nehru's pursuit of non-alignment enabled him to
be more truly catholic in outlook and contacts than might
otherwise have been the case. He could travel and have
discussions wherever he wished without offending the susceptibilities of this or that alliance or grouping. At heart he was a
true internationalist. It must have seemed incongruous to many
people that Nehru should have chosen the moment when
civil strife in India was rising ominously to inaugurate, on
March 23, 1947, in New Delhi, the first Asian Relations Conference. The gulf between Hindus and Moslems was visibly
widening, and the stage was inexorably being set for the
sanguinary clash that was to burst out later in that year. Yet,
amid every sign of impending tragedy, Nehru chose to launch
a conference to emphasise the unity of Asia. The gathering
itself achieved little, and those who (like the present writer)
saw the conference in session might have been pardoned if they
considered it a waste of time. But it marked a break with the
past, and in particular a break with Asia's subservience to
Europe and the West. And this was what Nehru intended it

should do. It also made it easier for India two years later to convene and act as host to a second conference of Asian states, the purpose of which was to secure the independence of the Dutch East Indies, now Indonesia. In these early years of his rule, Nehru succeeded by such conferences and by his visits around the world in winning a position of great prestige in international affairs both for his country and for himself as its leader. Since those early days of independence, New Delhi—with its imposing buildings and well-equipped halls and hotels—has become one of the world's main meeting places. For the rest of his life Nehru continued energetically to stride the international stage, and almost up to the moment of his death he hoped to pay another visit to London.

But, significantly, at the Bandung Conference held in 1955, Chou En-lai by all accounts was one of the figures whose debating skill and powers of exposition most impressed the delegates. The year before Pandit Nehru had visited China and had met Chou, and for the moment all seemed well between them. Though there was generally reported to be some rivalry between the Indian and Chinese delegations, the two countries had signed the famous agreement on Tibet which incorporated *Panch Shila*. But there is some evidence that Chou had certain border problems well in mind which he was anxious some time to discuss with Nehru—though for the present they might wait. In fact, it was not until 1960, five years after Bandung, that Chou En-lai came to the point during a visit to Delhi. After his talks he returned to Peking via Khatmandu where he held a press conference at which he is reported to have made the following remarks:

The statement Prime Minister Nehru made on the 26th February in parliament was not so friendly towards China. The statement I made at the press conference in Delhi on the evening of the 25th was very friendly towards India. But how did Prime Minister Nehru treat us? He did not say it face to face, but as soon as we left he attacked the Chinese Government as an aggressor. That is not an attitude to take towards guests. We were very much distressed by such an attitude, particularly because we respect Prime Minister Nehru.

With these words the first shots had been fired in the Indo-China border dispute.

Making due allowance for Chou's well-simulated sorrow that he had been so shabbily treated by a friend, there is no doubt that had Nehru accepted the fact that certain awkward matters were outstanding between India and China, that they were unlikely to be resolved by *Panch Shila* but might be susceptible to negotiation, there was just a chance that the border conflict and defeat of 1962 might have been avoided. Bandung produced a kind of euphoria which was dangerous to a person of Nehru's temperament. It papered over the cracks of Sino-Indian difficulties and served to disguise the hostility of Indonesia towards India, which later began to emerge.

However mistaken some of Nehru's premises in the field of foreign policy may later have proved, it is important to bear in mind one of his governing principles: the determination not to accept without question the validity of the assumptions upon which the post-war world had divided itself. The practical choices of a foreign policy which were open to India were limited: it could join one of the two major power blocs, Western or Communist, or pursue a policy of non-alignment with either. It chose the latter and has therefore been a neutral in the 'cold war'. India's position in this respect has not always been clearly understood. Its northern borders run in close proximity to territories that are under the direct rule of, or strongly influenced by, the two great Communist powers; the country's development plans call for a long period of peace; and India has an exaggerated fear of being dragged into someone else's war by regional pacts. Though now rapidly waning, the Congress Party's belief in passive resistance and the non-violent settlement of disputes, together with the foregoing factors, pointed to non-alignment as a practical basis for a foreign policy for independent India.

And in at least one important respect it can be claimed that non-alignment succeeded; it enabled India to accept aid without strings from both sides in the cold war. The policy of non-alignment was in operation so sincere and plain for all to see, that both America and Russia have been able to give the country substantial quantities of economic aid without any kind of political embarrassment. The first commitment of Soviet aid

started with the visit of Bulganin and Khrushchev to India in
1955, and ten years ago it was being freely prophesied that this
was the beginning of a process of sovietisation of the Indian
economy. Nothing of the sort has, of course, happened and for
the past decade both the United States and the Soviet Union
have been providing assistance for India in increasing quantities.
Nehru's foreign policy also moved India steadily towards
friendship with the Soviet Union: a friendship which India
valued for its own sake as well as for the link it gave with a
power which (until recently at any rate) was credited with
having considerable influence with China. Indeed, the development of a stable Indo-Soviet relationship can be claimed as one
of the positive achievements of Nehru's foreign policy, and
leads to the reflection that on the whole he was probably more
successful in his dealings with the non-Asian world than with
the Asian nations, assuming that for this purpose we count the
Soviet Union as part of Europe.

In these formative years relations with the United States of
America suffered a good many ups and downs, and probably
reached a high point during the Eisenhower administration.
America has been the principal source of aid for India's five
year plans, and for its help Nehru, like the rest of his countrymen, was duly grateful. But, while acknowledging America's
leadership of the free world, Nehru was at times suspicious of
its policies and was rarely prepared to go all the way in their
support. Nonetheless, throughout the Nehru premiership
relations between the two countries grew steadily more intimate
and each year sees some increase in the areas of affairs in which
they are mutually involved. Apart from aid, the USA now has a
significant commercial investment in India—in fact it is next to
the United Kingdom in the list of foreign investors.

The idea of India as a 'bridge' between East and West
implies some kind of special insight on the part of India into
the problems and aspirations of both hemispheres. It is an
idea which is easier to state than to define in the precise terms of
a foreign policy. But when Indians claim that their country
is a bridge between Asia and the West, they do not mean that
in some way it mediates between the two, though they would
probably say that Nehru more than anyone else helped the
West to understand (and to accept) the post-war political

awakening of Asia. They have in mind the fact that, through the British connection, they had more than two hundred years of contact with European thought and achievement; that they have assimilated more European political, administrative, scientific and other basic concepts than any other Asians; and that their non-attachment to either of the two great ideologies enables them to speak frankly to both. In effect, they are evolving a synthesis in the conduct of their affairs; planning, regulated by parliamentary democracy, which borrows its techniques from both the totalitarian states and the democracies, is an example. Nehru himself was, of course, a product of both East and West, but it is improbable that he would have claimed for India in its role of 'bridge builder' anything more esoteric than is stated above. There are some Indians who maintain that their country is not sufficiently identified in world affairs with Asia, where its true destiny must lie. Be that as it may, it is an undoubted advantage that there is one leading Asian power which can speak to the West in language it understands. Despite discouragements, India has always supported the proposal for the admission of the People's Republic of China to the United Nations, which it believes is not fully representative of world opinion as long as the most populous Asian nation is excluded from membership. There is no evidence that Nehru seriously contemplated the creation of a third force in international affairs; but in season and out he demanded recognition that Asia was now free and its countries no longer pawns in the game of European power politics. His support of the Chinese case at the UN reflects his feelings on this matter.

6

INDIA AND ITS
NEIGHBOURS

FROM THE BRIEF SURVEY given in the previous chapter of
Nehru's role in general international affairs, we now pass on to
consider his approach to some of the more difficult aspects of
Indian foreign policy: the relations between India and its
neighbours. In this chapter we look at Nehru's policy in regard
to the Kashmir problem, to the European enclaves in the subcontinent, and to Ceylon and Burma. In the next chapter an
outline is given of Sino-Indian relations since independence and
of India's relations with the Himalayan border states of Nepal,
Bhutan and Sikkim.

Pakistan

Of all the external problems facing the new India in 1947, the
most complex and acute was the establishing of some kind of
working arrangement with Pakistan, which many Indians—
and not Indians alone—found difficult to regard as a foreign
country. There was a tendency, especially in the broad Hindi-
speaking belt of central India, to regard Pakistan as a sort of
inferior India and this, probably more than anything else, made
relations between the two countries difficult from the beginning.
On top of this one had to set the rending of old Hindu and
Moslem family friendships that went back generations. The
prospects were not favourable, though one would have thought
that good mutual relations would have been at the top of the
list of foreign policy priorities of two close neighbours jointly
occupying the subcontinental land mass and enjoying a shared

political and cultural history—not to mention a marked degree of economic interdependence. But not so: the operation of amputating Pakistan from the body of India left too many scars and exposed nerves for relations between the two countries to start on a normal plane. Nehru had many Moslem friends—mostly intellectuals—but it is to be doubted whether he ever understood the deep feeling of the Moslem masses as they watched the rise of Hindu influence while the British began progressively to demit office and responsibility. A pithy and sympathetic definition of what Pakistan is and what it stands for, is given by Ian Stephens: 'The idea was to provide a home-land for the subcontinent's Muslims, or most of them; a place where, after the British imperial power had gone, they could freely develop their way of life in an Islamic environment apart from the Hindus, who outnumbered them by about three to one.'[1]

The causes of the ill-feeling between India and Pakistan are not so numerous as is sometimes imagined, but none of them is unimportant and all of them have so far proved more or less intractable. They cannot all of them be examined in detail in these pages, but we may note a few of the chief ones. They are: the problem of the division of the head waters of the Indus, on which the irrigation systems of northern India and West Pakistan depend; the allegedly unfair division of assets which Pakistan declares took place at the time of the partition; outstanding claims in regard to refugee property in both countries; unsatisfactory economic relationships; and the problem of Kashmir. Of these, the last named is by far the most important, and it is probable that if only Kashmir could be 'settled' all the other outstanding Indo-Pakistani problems would fall into place. It is certainly one of the most persistent of all the international problems of our time, and has been on the agenda of the Security Council of the United Nations on more than one hundred occasions since India first brought the issue to the Council's attention on January 1, 1948. A five-member United Nations Commission on India and Pakistan (UNCIP) was then appointed. It secured a ceasefire which became effective on January 1, 1949. A member of the Commission, Josef Korbel, offers an explanation of the tense feeling which continues to exist between the two countries.

The real cause of all the bitterness and bloodshed, all the venomed speech, the recalcitrance and the suspicion that have characterised the Kashmir dispute is the uncompromising and perhaps uncompromisable struggle of two ways of life, two concepts of political organisation, two scales of values, two spiritual attitudes, that find themselves locked in deadly conflict in which Kashmir has become both symbol and battleground. Simply, these two irrevocably opposed positions may be characterised thus: To India the subcontinent is inescapably one nation. To Pakistan it is just as inescapably two.[2]

It is doubtful if Nehru realised the extent of the support among Moslems for the 'two nations theory', as it came to be called. A state based upon theocratic foundations was something which was repugnant to his agnostic mind and rationalist outlook. Nevertheless, he and the other Congress leaders grudgingly agreed to partition as part of the price to be paid for independence. Only C. Rajagopalachari, veteran Congress leader and now head of the Swatantra Party, advocated a settlement with the Moslems—if need be by the division of the subcontinent; but he received no thanks for his wise and (in the circumstances of the time) courageous words. The origins of the Kashmir dispute are too complicated to be traced in detail here, but it is necessary to say briefly how the affair began, how it has developed, and to offer some observations on the latest turn of events in this tragic story.

The arrangements made for the future of the five-hundred-odd Princely States were perhaps the most vulnerable part of the scheme for the transfer of power from British to Indian hands. The plans for the Princes which the departing administration produced were the least satisfactory part of their programme and it was not until July 25, 1947, three weeks before India became an independent sovereign state, that Earl Mountbatten disclosed his scheme for the future of the Princely States. At this last meeting of the Chamber of Princes he told the rulers that with independence the doctrine of paramountcy would lapse, i.e. their treaties with the paramount power (the British government) would be at an end. Technically and legally they would all be independent, but as some of the smaller states were no bigger than Hyde Park, this was not a very comforting prospect to their rulers or their subjects. But Mountbatten pointed out that, as the Princely States were indissolubly part of the Indian subcontinent, they would require some kind of formal association with one or other of the Dominions that were about to replace the British Raj. For that purpose they would be given an instrument of accession, which would enable them to 'accede' to either the Dominion of India or the Dominion of Pakistan in respect of defence, external affairs and communications. There would be no financial or other involvement and, said Earl Mountbatten, 'my scheme leaves you with all the practical independence you can use and makes you free of all those subjects which you cannot possibly manage on your own'. Mountbatten's statement has been much criticised yet, taken as a whole, his plan, in this writer's opinion, amounted to something far better than the slow-moving and ultra-conservative Political Department, whose main desire was to preserve the status quo, was ever likely to produce—if, indeed, it could have produced anything at all.

It had been made clear at the meeting on July 25 that, subject to geographical considerations, States would choose which of the two Dominions they wished to adhere to. This left considerable scope for disputation, as several States had frontiers which abutted on to both Dominions. Among these was the State of Kashmir. Moslems comprised three quarters of its population, but politically it was controlled by a high-cast Hindu maharajah and a Brahmin elite, from which class Nehru's family sprang.*

For the purposes of 'accession', Kashmir was a State exposed to powerful influences in both directions. The fact that, of the $4\frac{1}{2}$ million inhabitants of Kashmir and Jammu, the great majority were Moslems (descendants of fourteenth-century converts) could be held as a valid reason for joining them with their co-religionists in Pakistan. On the other hand, the one quarter of the population which was Hindu provided the administration, such as it was, and most of Kashmir's tenuous economic links with the outside world. Furthermore, by the Treaty of Amritsar signed with the British in 1846, Kashmir

* I reject the view held by some people that this had any material bearing on the Indian prime minister's reaction to subsequent events.

was to belong 'forever, an independent possession, to Maharajah Gulab Singh and the heirs male of his body'. Gulab Singh was a much more redoubtable figure than the last maharajah, H. H. Sir Hari Singh Bahadur, who ascended the *gadi* in 1925 to live out to its end a dynasty that had governed poorly, even by the standards of 'Princely India'.

By 1947 the position was very roughly that, on a counting of heads, there was a good case for accession to Pakistan; against this could be set the undoubted fact that there was strong legal, and some practical, support for accession to India. In such an evenly balanced situation, Hari Singh was not the man to make a quick or clear-cut decision. Quite the contrary; it was eminently congenial to him to temporise with difficulties. So he moved himself into what he thought was an impregnably neutral position. On August 12, 1947, he declared that he intended to conclude a standstill agreement with both India and Pakistan which would preserve some of the *status quo*. In an address to the East India Association after his return from India, Lord Mountbatten described the matter in these words:

> In the case of Kashmir I went up personally and saw the Maharajah. I spent four days with him in July and on every one of these four days I persisted with the same advice. 'Ascertain the will of your people by any means and join whichever Dominion your people wish to join by August 13 this year.' He did not do that, and what happened can be seen. Had he acceded to Pakistan before August 14 the future government of India had allowed me to give His Highness an assurance that no objection would be raised by them. Had His Highness acceded to India by August 14 Pakistan did not then exist, and therefore could not have interfered. The only trouble that could have been raised was by non-accession to either side, and this was unfortunately the very course followed by the Maharajah.[3]

Immediately after the transfer of power, Lord Ismay (who was assisting Mountbatten) visited Kashmir to try to persuade the maharajah to make up his mind one way or the other, but to no avail.

Such were the simple facts of the Kashmir situation at the

time of independence. There were many personal, political and religious overtones which need not detain us here. But two circumstances in particular should be mentioned. First, Pakistan accepted the standstill agreement but India gave no definite reply.* Secondly, throughout the summer of 1947 the Kashmir government had been having a good deal of trouble with its Moslem subjects in the province of Poonch. For these the accession question presented no doubts or difficulties. Their desire that Kashmir should join up with Pakistan was greatly heightened by reports (whether ill or well founded) of Hindu atrocities in the general exodus of Moslems from India and by the arrival on the Kashmir scene of Moslem tribesmen from the North-West Frontier. These tribesmen—traditionally never slow in taking an opportunity to loot, pillage, rape or murder the infidel—poured into Kashmir. Behaving with the utmost savagery they swept on to a point about twenty miles from Srinagar from which the maharajah and his much-shaken administration were endeavouring to maintain a semblance of authority. The maharajah's own forces proved quite unable to stem the torrent of invasion and brutality. Law and order broke down completely and effective government disappeared. In this situation and believing that the tribesmen were being encouraged and helped by Pakistan, which also, it was alleged, was holding up essential supplies of such things as petrol and salt routed through Pakistan, the maharajah appealed to India for military and civil aid.

Delhi held that it could help Kashmir only if the State acceded to India. Accordingly an Instrument of Accession was signed on October 26, 1947. At first light the following morning, October 27, an airlift of Indian troops into Kashmir began. In accepting the accession, Lord Mountbatten, governor-general of the Dominion of India, wrote to Maharajah Hari Singh:[6] . . . it is my Government's wish that as soon as law and order have been restored in Kashmir and its soil cleared of the invader, the

---

* Cf. V. P. Menon, *The Story of the Integration of the States*, Longmans, London, 1956, p. 395: 'We left the State alone. We did not ask the Maharajah to accede . . . our hands were already full and, if the truth be told, I for one had simply no time to think of Kashmir.' Menon was secretary to the States Ministry which was the successor to the Foreign and Political Department of British India.

question of the State's accession should be settled by reference to its people'.

In fact, the invader has never wholly been cleared from the soil of Kashmir, and in consequence no reference has been made to the people regarding its accession to India. Indian troops reached the heights of Uri by November 11. By that time the tribesmen to all intents and purposes were beaten, and the Indian army was able to establish and hold a front running roughly on the line of Kotli-Poonch-Uri. Opposed to them were the 'Azad' Kashmir army and units of the Pakistan army; these moved into position early in 1948. There were no pitched battles, but desultory patrol actions continued throughout the year until, largely as a result of the mediation of the United Nations Commission, a cease-fire became effective on the first day of 1949.

Under the formula agreed, Pakistan was to control areas to the west and north of the cease-fire line, which included the western sections of the provinces of Jammu, Poonch and Kashmir, and also the northern territories of Gilgit and Baltistan. India was to receive a larger share of both Jammu and Kashmir (including Srinagar and the Valley) as well as the Buddhist province of Ladakh, east of the Pir Panjal mountains— an area which has since figured prominently in another department of India's foreign policy. Both governments agreed to accept two resolutions dated August 13, 1948, and January 5, 1949, which provided the outline of a settlement by demilitarising the State of Jammu and Kashmir and enabling the population to determine its future status through a free and impartial plebiscite. Technically, the cease-fire line of the armistice of 1949 still apportions their respective parts of Kashmir to India and Pakistan. Until August 1965 their forces observed an armed and uneasy truce which served to conceal deep and dangerous feelings.

The area controlled by India is now officially recognised as a member state of the Indian Union; that controlled by Pakistan is known as 'Azad' (or 'free') Kashmir, while Gilgit and Baltistan, also under Pakistan's surveillance, are for convenience known as the Northern Territories. The numerous references of the question to the Security Council, the heavy barrage of words from both sides of the border and the constant outpouring of

D

charges and counter-charges over the years (including shrill cries of genocide) have made it extremely difficult for all but the most informed specialist to keep track of the tangled skein of the controversy.[4] When the cease-fire had been negotiated, the Security Council sought unsuccessfully to begin a programme of demilitarisation as a prelude to a plebiscite. The Indian case has always been that the maharajah's accession was legal and binding; that in consequence the presence of Indian troops in Kashmir could not be questioned; that in entering Kashmir in support of the tribesmen, Pakistan's forces had committed an aggression, and that until this was put right Delhi was not prepared to acknowledge that Pakistan had any *locus standi* in the dispute. Addressing the Security Council on October 7, 1957, the Indian representative, Krishna Menon, said:

> There is a difference between India and Pakistan in relation to the India Act (1947). We are the successor state, the Government of India . . . the legitimate successor of British authority in India. . . . We have taken over all the liabilities . . . therefore, even without any succession, we have the obligation to go to the rescue of these people.

This was a more comprehensive claim than any that had previously been made, and the writer is not competent to pronounce on its validity in international law. But as the quarrel dragged on and the positions of the respective protagonists hardened, India and Nehru came to rely less upon purely legalistic points and more upon the practical politics of the affair.

Notwithstanding the 1947 partition, some 45 million Moslems had remained behind in India and 9 million Hindus had stayed on in Pakistan, overwhelmingly concentrated in the east wing of that country. These minorities were in a special sense hostages to fortune and to the good behaviour and tolerance of the majority community. Nehru, at least, was always very conscious that a false move over Kashmir might spark off a communal explosion, which he might not be able to control, against the Indian Moslems. Indeed, in the early part of 1964, just before his death, there were signs of increasing restiveness in East Pakistan and West Bengal, which in the past had experienced several waves of mass migration between the two arcas. Nehru's very real concern about its communal implications sometimes induced in him an attitude of apparent inaction over Kashmir, and a reluctance to reopen questions which he thought were best left alone. It was as though he were content to leave everything as it was and hope for the best. But towards the end of his life the enmity of China and India's military reverse in the 'frontier war' forced some reconsideration of the Kashmir question. One of his last major acts was to order the release from detention (since 1953) of his old friend Sheikh Abdullah, the leader of the Kashmir National Conference, and cancel his trial, which had been proceeding at a leisurely pace for some months.

India has invested a great deal of money and prestige in the part of Kashmir under its control. This has done much for its long-term economic development, particularly in the field of communications. India's heavy military expenditure in the area has brought an additional measure of prosperity to the people of the State. Whether all this has added to the sum total of the happiness of the Indian people, including those of Kashmir, is another matter. In reply to allegations that politics in Indian-controlled Kashmir are corrupt and that the elections for the State assembly are rigged, India points to Pakistan's own electoral record, claiming that this puts it in no position to criticise. But there were signs which suggested that, at the time of his death, Nehru might have been moving cautiously towards the idea of a settlement. It would seem that, to be acceptable to Pakistan, any such agreement must involve some sacrifice of Indian sovereignty, however small. Jawaharlal Nehru was probably the only Indian statesman who would have been able to make any such proposition acceptable to his people. His immediate successor, the late Lal Bahadur Shastri, needed time to build up his position. The same problem may well face the new leader, Indira Gandhi. Shastri's brief call on President Ayub Khan in October 1964 seemed to break the ice. But with China meddling in the dispute, relations grew worse, and war broke out between India and Pakistan in summer 1965. Then, tragically, when Russian initiative brought them together at Tashkent in January 1966, Shastri's sudden death confronted India once more with a leadership problem.

The developments which took place within twenty months of

Nehru's death have made the possibility of an Indo-Pakistan settlement even more remote than before. During the early summer of 1965, a disagreement arose regarding the exact location of that sector of the Indo-Pakistan frontier which passes through the part of the desolate swamp bordering the Arabian Sea, known as the Rann of Kutch. Presumably the area may be regarded as having some strategic significance for neighbours whose relations are permanently tense and touchy. A certain amount of skirmishing by patrols on both sides took place and there were some casualties. More important was the ugly temper which the affair revealed. British policy was to get the two sides to the conference table, and eventually, by the effort of the British high commissioners in New Delhi and Karachi (aided by the approaching monsoon which annually inundates the Rann to about knee-depth), an agreement was reached and signed on June 30 providing for a cease fire, a rapid withdrawal of troops, reversion to the position obtaining at December 31, 1964, an early meeting at ministerial level and, failing a settlement by mutual agreement within a period of two months, an acceptance of settlement by mediation.

Mr Shastri had no easy task in defending India's acceptance of the truce in parliament, some of whose members professed their inability to grasp the difference between mediation, arbitration and adjudication. The spirit of the agreement did not, however, survive for very long. In the third week of August it was announced that India had asked Pakistan to cancel the meeting of the foreign ministers which had by then been arranged to discuss Kutch border problems. The reason given was that there was little likelihood of an agreement in view of the deteriorating relations between the two countries. So far as India was concerned the question could be referred at once to a tribunal, for which provision was contained in the cease-fire agreement. Indeed, even in the short period of the Kutch imbroglio, relations between the two countries had slumped disastrously. Kutch might be regarded as just another tiresome item in the lengthy list of Indo-Pakistan differences, but it was soon overshadowed by military action on a much larger canvas which was to cause acute anxiety in Delhi. Once more there were bonnets over the Kashmir border, this time on a big enough scale to engulf the entire subcontinent, if the flames of war were not quickly extinguished.

Chronological exactitude about events taking place by stealth several thousand miles away is not always possible, but from about mid-July, India was complaining of border violations by armed 'infiltrators', actively aided by the Pakistani authorities. The Pakistan case was that the movement was a spontaneous uprising of the people of Kashmir against the Indian occupier; that it was led by 'freedom fighters' supported by Azad (Pakistan-held) Kashmir forces; and that, as Pakistan had given a solemn pledge to the people of Kashmir, it had a clear duty to lend support to its co-religionists. In whatever way this latest episode may have begun, the plain fact is that by the end of August 1965 the two countries were at war in all but name; massive movements of troops had begun, air and tank battles had been fought and the conflict was particularly fierce in the Chhamb area which commands the new all-weather Jammu-Poonch road, the main supply route for Indian forces in Kashmir State. According to official Indian sources, during August about 450 Pakistan raiders bodies had been counted while it was estimated that another 500 had been killed, and more than a hundred Pakistani prisoners had been taken. The first days of September brought still bloodier fighting with a correspondingly higher total of dead and wounded. (This and subsequent developments are discussed at greater length in the Postscript.)

Kashmir was not, of course, the only subject on which Indian policy had departed widely from that pursued by Pakistan. Religious differences may lie at the root of the Kashmir quarrel and may well be the reason for its continuance; but between two neighbours who have many mutual commercial interests the religious factor should not obtrude into such a matter as the external value of their common currency, the rupee. Yet for a time there was considerable rivalry between the two rupees— a rivalry which seemed to be grounded on sentiment rather than on hard facts and the highly technical considerations which should determine the external parity of a currency. India and Pakistan are both in the sterling area, all the member countries of which decided to devalue their currencies under Britain's

initiative in September 1949—all, that is, except Pakistan. This
placed the Pakistan rupee at a premium over the Indian
rupee, and Indo-Pakistan trade was brought to a virtual standstill (with acute shortages of raw jute and cotton for the Indian
mills, which were living in a veritable state of seige for several
months). Then in 1951 India wisely decided to recognise the
higher parity of the Pakistani rupee, and the International
Monetary Fund also gave its blessing to Pakistan's higher rate,
which lasted a further four years until 1955. Pakistan was greatly
helped by the effect of the Korean War on the prices of primary
products: a circumstance which could not possibly have been
foreseen when in 1949 it decided against devaluation and in
favour of the higher rate.

At partition the hope was that, at least in the sphere of
finance and trade, the two Dominions would start with a clean
sheet. In December 1947, an Indo-Pakistan Financial Settlement had been initialled under which Pakistan was to receive
Rs 75 crores as its share of undivided India's cash balances,
Rs 20 crores of which had been paid over on the day of partition. It was also agreed that both Dominions should have a
common currency system and a common central bank until the
end of March 1948. Neither materialised and the Trade
Standstill Agreement was denounced by India after Pakistan
imposed an export duty on jute. Such was the sorry tale of the
first proposals for trade and banking between the two countries.
The creation of something like tolerable commercial conditions
between two adjoining nations, who should in fact be close and
friendly partners, has been a long and exhausting business,
and one owing more to the skill and patience of senior civil
servants than to the wisdom of politicians.

The division of the waters of the river Indus and its five
tributaries has been another subject of recurring dispute between
the two countries. The Sutlej, the Beas, the Ravi, the Chenab
and the Jhelum rivers pour their waters into the Indus, and
their smooth and uninterrupted flow is of supreme importance
to the economies of both India and Pakistan. Counting Indians
and Pakistanis together, some 40 million people live in the
Indus Basin area. Thus, for both countries the supply of water
is a life-and-death issue in a way that nations whose rivers run

their full course under a single sovereignty find difficult to appreciate. The Boundary Commission, which delimited the northern frontier between India and Pakistan in 1947, did not greatly concern itself with the circumstance that the line it drew cut right across a complicated system of rivers and canals which constituted part of the life-blood of two new nations. The Commission's chairman, Lord (then Sir Cyril) Radcliffe, thought he 'was entitled to assume that any agreement . . . as to the sharing of the waters from the canals (forming part of the irrigation system of the Indus Basin) or otherwise will be respected by whatever government hereafter assumes jurisdiction over the headwork concerned'.

It was a big and, as events showed, a rash assumption. There was a standstill agreement which provided for no change up to March 31, 1948, in the proportion of water that had previously been allowed to flow downstream into Pakistan. A few weeks later a new agreement was entered into, which India claimed was designed to give Pakistan time to tap alternative sources. However, as the Pakistanis had made no effort in this respect by September, India threatened to cut off supplies altogether to the two principal canals connecting the Indus waters to Pakistan. Nehru then personally intervened and the threat was withdrawn; but it was made clear that in this sector supplies of water would be progressively reduced from the Indian end. The seeds of another serious quarrel had thus been sown; indeed, many people regarded the dispute over the Indus Basin as being potentially quite as dangerous as Kashmir. Access to water to irrigate the land whose crops maintain human and animal life was a good deal more fundamental to people's needs than the refinements of the argument as to who fired the first shots in Kashmir. For a time the situation was tense, and matters were brought to a head by a serious drought in the winter of 1952–3 which created a shortage of water for both countries. The situation was aggravated by allegations that India was deliberately taking more than its agreed share out of the Indus Basin, and thus keeping Pakistan permanently in short supply. Though this charge was never proved, it was never withdrawn.

In the meantime the World Bank had agreed to try to bring about a settlement of the dispute. After hearing irreconcilable claims from the two governments, the Bank put forward proposals of its own. These had the merit of lifting the quarrel out of its political context and treating it as a practical problem susceptible of a practical solution. The officials of the World Bank made it clear that it was not to be settled by the promulgation of a juridical award, and in the event an agreement was achieved from which neither side could claim to have gained a 'victory' over the other. The only victory was for reasonableness and common sense, and it was achieved by a World Bank team led by Sir William Iliffe, which showed great patience over a period of some seven years as well as an imaginative understanding of the needs of both parties. The agreement was in due course elevated to the status of a treaty, of which the centre-piece was a division of the waters on the basis that the three eastern rivers (Sutlej, Beas and Ravi) should be for the use of India, leaving the three western rivers (Indus, Jhelum and Chenab) for the use of Pakistan. To transfer water from the three western rivers to meet irrigation needs in those parts of Pakistan which have hitherto depended on supplies from the three eastern rivers, it is necessary to construct new works which will cost something like Rs 500 crores (roughly £350 million or $1,000 million), partly in foreign exchange and partly in local currencies. Large-scale financial assistance has been mobilised by the World Bank and the work is already in hand. The effect of the new arrangement has been to release the entire flow of the three eastern rivers for irrigation development in India, and in recognition of this India has joined the financial consortium which is supporting the scheme.

To a large extent, helpful World Bank intervention removed the sting from the Indus waters' dispute, but there remain other issues which continue to keep open the wounds that were created by partition and the events immediately following. Perhaps the most important are questions still outstanding which relate to the disposal of refugee property—most of it immovable, and therefore not transferable even if normal commercial intercourse were to exist between the two countries. Generally speaking, in the vast migrations which preceded and accompanied independence and have occurred since (which some authorities estimate have displaced as many as 20 million people), losses of property have been heaviest amongst Hindus leaving Pakistan for India and least amongst Moslems proceeding from India to Pakistan.

The reason for this is simple; by and large, in the pre-independence subcontinent the Hindu was the capitalist, the investor and the man of property—though, of course, there were also millions of Hindus who were fated to a life cycle of poverty and debt, never possessing more than a few rupees; but in so far as there was a property-owning rentier class, it was predominantly Hindu. Few Moslems still had a stake in industry or such activities as banking, which the Hindu had always regarded as a strategically important area of the economy. The result was that, in the successive waves of refugees which passed over the Indo-Pakistan frontiers from 1947 onwards, the losses by Hindus tended to be greater in terms of money value than the losses of Moslems, who were chiefly small-scale cultivators and traders.

Both governments set up organisations for the custody of evacuee property; but in the first phase of partition they had their hands full with the reception and resettlement of the refugees—a process which has gone on intermittently ever since. There have been innumerable conferences and discussions at ministerial and official level, and plentiful exchanges of memoranda, but all to no avail. All efforts at a comprehensive settlement have proved abortive. Under any formula it is almost certain that Pakistan would have to make much the larger compensation payment to India, and has therefore no great inducement to speed up a settlement. In the meantime, of course, it is people rather than institutions that are mainly affected, and to them the sense of loss is personal and individual. Many of the affected parties have died and others have grown old and bitter while waiting. On any practical view, it is now most unlikely that the owners of evacuee property will ever receive any compensation, and the whole thing has perhaps now to be regarded as a lost cause which has further soured the dealings between the two countries.

Kashmir and economic questions do not by any means exhaust the catalogue of subjects on which there are serious differences between India and Pakistan. But there are some mitigating factors. The unhappy memories of the late 1940s are fading and a new generation is growing up. Both countries have found their respective places in the scheme of things and have settled down to a separate but purposeful programme of work. Only Kashmir remains as a constant irritant and potential source of hostilities. In both countries the minorities continue to be apprehensive, but their condition is by no means parlous. Indeed, one of the redeeming features of the open war between India and Pakistan which flared out in 1965 was that there were no reprisals against the religious minority in either country and no outbreaks of communal strife between Hindus and Moslems.

With his unquestionably sincere concern for the position of the Moslems in India, Nehru combined rigidity towards Pakistan—a state which had been brought into being to satisfy the demands of the subcontinent's largest and most clamant minority. The territorial integrity and natural unity of India had always been an article of faith in pre-independence nationalist politics, and many Indians consider that by agreeing to the partitioning of the country they made a very considerable sacrifice which has gone unrequited and which Pakistanis have never recognised. Indians are certainly unwilling to see any further dismemberment of their country, and quite apart from the legal aspects of the matter (where India appears to be on strong ground), this would seem to be one of the main reasons for their apparently unyielding stand over Kashmir. Indeed, Nehru's policy to Kashmir received confirmation by L. B. Shastri, whose government in December 1964 took steps towards the closer integration of the State into the Indian Union by extending to it the provisions of Articles 356 and 357 of the Indian Constitution. These enable the central government in certain circumstances to proclaim presidential rule in a State and authorise the Indian parliament to enact laws for it. India has thus tightened its grip on Kashmir, and so there seems little likelihood in the near future of a peaceful settlement of this key problem in Indo-Pakistani relations. The peace moves which many people think Nehru was considering at the time of his death were soon dropped, and antagonisms increased to the point of armed conflict.

The European Enclaves

This theme of the territorial integrity of India has had its influence in other sectors of both foreign and domestic policy. European rivalries of the eighteenth century and even earlier were partly fought out in the Indian subcontinent where the British East India Company's armies, often with the aid of local Indian princes, scored notable victories over Dutch, Portuguese and French forces. By treaties made and signed in Europe and governed chiefly by European interests, the defeated powers were allowed to retain tiny portions of the Indian mainland. Pondicherry and Goa, with one or two smaller attached townships, were the two main coastal enclaves that remained at the time of independence.

It was clear to any observer looking with twentieth-century eyes that these old colonial enclaves could survive only by special arrangement with the successor government in Delhi, and that such an arrangement was most unlikely to be reached with an administration which regarded all relics of colonialism with extreme distaste. The French quickly realised the weakness of their position in Pondicherry and Chandernagore: colonial fragments which they had retained over the years more from sentimental reasons than from the practical advantages they brought. Accordingly, they took steps to negotiate a transfer of their Indian possessions to the Delhi government. Chandernagore was incorporated in India on June 9, 1952, while Pondicherry, Mahe, Karikal and Yanaon were transferred *de facto* on November 1, 1954 and formally ceded by treaty on May 28, 1956. The total area involved was less than 200 square miles.

The Portuguese, on the other hand, continued to treat Goa as an integral part of metropolitan Portugal. They had, it is true, been in Goa since the middle of the sixteenth century when they had made it into a thriving trading and missionary centre, associated throughout Christendom with the name of Saint Francis Xavier. But by the eighteenth century, the standing of Goa had declined sharply, and for the whole period of British rule in India it remained a sleepy, second-class port, handling chiefly export cargoes of iron ore. There was some smuggling and in the two world wars it caused a good deal of trouble to the British-Indian government by providing a hide-out for enemy shipping. After the second world war there were uncorroborated rumours that the Nizam of Hyderabad, who was still thinking in terms of an independent kingdom of Hyderabad and the Berars, would like an outlet to the sea and might make a deal with Portugal in respect to Goa. If true, the idea came to nothing.

Apart from the facts of geography, there was a strong ethnic and logical case for an approach by the Portuguese to the Indian government for a peaceful settlement of the future of Goa. There is also some evidence to suggest that Nehru expected and hoped for such an approach. For a long time the demand for a union of Goa with India was carried on by means of more or less peaceful political agitation. But by 1961 the situation along the frontier had become tense. There was to be a general election early in 1962, and inflammatory speeches were made alleging that Indians in Goa were suffering serious hardships and disabilities. The interest of the world press was aroused when Krishna Menon, Nehru's minister of Defence, declared that the matter should be settled once and for all, if necessary by force. Charges and counter-charges increasingly assumed the form that has become all too familiar as the prelude to 'lib-eration' operations. Nehru, who had for several years done his best to keep the dispute on a peaceful plane, finally lost patience. On December 18, 1961 the Indian army marched into Goa.

In spite of their earlier brave words, the Portuguese put up only a token resistance. In the West there was criticism of Nehru and a disposition to brand him as an aggressor; but throughout the Afro-Asian world his action was regarded as a fully justified final blow against colonialism. The pity is that, with a little more perception by the Portuguese of political realities, the affair might have been settled peacefully and in a manner that would have brought honour rather than humilia-tion to Portugal. Some of those who were in a position to observe Nehru at close quarters at this particular time consider that Goa represented the high point in an internal conflict he was experiencing: whether or not to resolve matters by force. It is perhaps not without significance that his first serious illness occurred in the spring of 1962, following upon Goa and a strenuous election campaign.

Ceylon

While India's post-independence relations with Ceylon have never looked like developing into anything more than a sharp verbal duel, they have nonetheless been a source of weakness and embarrassment to both countries. About the size of the Irish Republic, Ceylon is separated from the south-east tip of India by a stretch of shallow water, the Palk Strait, which at its narrowest point is forty miles across and at its widest eighty-five miles. That two such close neighbours with so much in common have failed to reach a working understanding about one of the big problems concerning them—the status of the Indian minority in Ceylon—is a sad commentary on the inability of men to manage their affairs in certain circumstances. Between 1901 and 1963, the population of Ceylon increased from 3½ to 10½ million, and the expectation of life at birth has more than doubled during the last forty years. By 1960 life-expectancy was estimated to have reached sixty-six years. Of the total population of 10½ million, approximately one million, or around ten per cent, are of Indian origin—either first generation immigrants or the descendants of Tamil and other workers who followed British capital and enterprise when the island was opened up in the second half of the nineteenth century. For a hundred years or more, with the virtually unhindered transit of men and money between India and Ceylon under the protecting shield of British authority, Indians in Ceylon suffered no disability and could come and go freely between Ceylon and their ancestral villages on the mainland, as well as make remittances to relatives and friends there. In the past, the easy-going Sinhalese were on the whole quite indifferent to the presence of a large force of alien labour in their midst. But the situation changed with independence and the growth of economic nationalism. Ceylon, already overpopulated, has an annual population increase running now at 2.8 per cent; large numbers of its citizens are unemployed and underemployed. In such a dilemma, the Sinhalese have become deeply resentful of the presence of the Tamil community.

Indo-Ceylonese relations since independence have been so far mainly a fruitless exercise in trying to endow the Indian minority in the island with a satisfactory status in one country or the other. The Indian case is that Indian nationals have made a sizeable contribution to the economic development of Ceylon, and hence the full right of Ceylonese citizenship should be granted to those Indians born and bred in the island who fulfil normal citizenship qualifications; residence permits should be given to those otherwise qualified. This would leave only a small residue of Indians whose expatriation to India would settle the problem for good. In 1953 Nehru and Dudley Senanayake used the opportunity of a Commonwealth Prime Minister's Conference in London to try to arrive at an agreed formula. The Indian understanding of the matter was that the Ceylonese prime minister undertook to accept 400,000 Indians as citizens of Ceylon and give permanent residence to another 250,000. Machinery was set up for dealing with Ceylonese citizenship for Indians and the repatriation of other Indians, but it has never worked. There has been constant disagreement over the statistics of the problem, each side claiming the right to interpret them its own way. Although Tamil has been acknowledged as an official language in certain areas, Sinhalese is still virtually the sole official language.

Though Pandit Nehru several times made an appeal for a settlement with the Ceylonese government, nothing very practical had been achieved by the time of his death. In October 1964 his successor, Lal Bahadur Shastri, had discussions in Colombo with Mrs Sirimavo Bandaranaike. At the end of these it was announced in a joint statement that, out of 975,000 affected persons, Ceylon would accept 300,000 as citizens of Ceylon and India 525,000 as citizens of India, the status of the remaining 150,000 persons of Indian origin to be settled in subsequent discussions. 'It was agreed that the admission to Ceylon citizenship of the 300,000 persons and the repatriation of the 525,000 persons should be spread over a period of 15 years and that the two processes should keep pace with each other.'

To the outsider it would seem that, by extending the implementation of the agreement over a decade-and-a-half, the probability of further delays and misunderstandings has been correspondingly increased. It is likely that the problem will remain unresolved for a long time to come. It is difficult to avoid the conclusion that, during the long period that this matter has been under discussion by the two governments, India's bargaining position has become progressively worse.

Burma

In spite of many protestations of close friendship between India and Burma (especially during U Nu's premiership), some idea of the hapless position of Indians in that country may be inferred from the fact that during 1964 the Indian government had to make special arrangements to evacuate from Burma by sea and air large numbers of Indians. These have lost their property and their livelihood as a result of the progressive socialisation of Burmese commerce and industry, and the relentless pursuit of economic nationalism. The present predicament of the Indian minority is not wholly to be laid at the door of the Delhi administration, though it can be held against the Indian government that it never really appreciated that a Burma fully separated from India (the severance in 1937 retained a link with India by way of British rule in both countries) might also be an unfriendly Burma. Writing in 1942, G. E. Harvey, a distinguished civil servant who knew Burma well, noted:

There were one million Indians in Burma. They constituted an acute problem, and it was our [i.e. British] doing. There had always been Indians, but never in such large numbers until we introduced them. . . . When they followed us to Burma, Indians already had a couple of centuries start over the Burman. They had the good-will of our trade, they handled the new business we introduced, they took charge of the money-lending, and for long they monopolised the professions, legal, medical, accountancy, engineering, as no Burman was qualified. . . . And they swamped the labour market, arriving annually by sea. . . . They came for the work, the high wages of a new and thinly populated land. Their remittances home probably reached £5 million a year.[5]

It has been truly said that, economically speaking, Burma was much more a dependency of India than of Britain. The ubiquitous money-lenders, who financed the rice crop and were traditionally supposed to prey on the cultivator, were Chettiars from south India: efficient, immensely patient and, when necessary, quite ruthless. At the time of the Japanese occupation probably four-fifths of the agricultural debt of Burma was owed to Chettiars—a debt subsequently cancelled at a stroke of the pen by an edict of the Rangoon government. Clearly, when the Burmese consider India, they have much to remember and brood on.

Many Indians left Burma when the Japanese advanced on the country in 1942; some remained throughout the wartime occupation; others returned when Burma attained independence on January 4, 1948. It is difficult to say with any degree of accuracy what number of Indians survived the vicissitudes of war, civil disorder and an economic policy manifestly devised to put all non-Burmans out of business and work in Burma. A census of 1953 reported that there were about 800,000 Indians and Pakistanis in the country, of which the great majority would almost certainly be Indians. Under the new regime their lot has been far from easy and they have been treated as second-class citizens in a country where they have made substantial investments in money and skills.

Burmese opinion of the outside world tends to vary with the price of rice, for which India has always been one of Burma's chief customers. With the post-war food situation almost always precarious in India and rice fluctuating in price between £40 and £80 a ton, Burma has generally possessed a strong bargaining weapon. Neither an Indian loan of Rs 20 crores (£15 million) negotiated in 1956, nor India's earlier cancellation of Burma's outstanding debt of Rs 45 crores (£33¾ million) arising from the financial terms of the 1937 separation, has served to soften the heart of the Burmese administration towards India.

Over recent years the Rangoon government has been moving steadily in the direction of the Communist bloc. A thousand miles of Burma's land frontier marches with China and the Burmese have to tread warily in the shadow of their powerful eastern neighbour. In spite of much shared idealism between Nehru and U Nu when the latter was in office, and in spite of past commercial links and present needs, it is questionable if India has exercised any real influence over Burmese policy, either internal or external. So far as concerns Burma, it must be said that Pandit Nehru's policies failed to win friends and influence people.

India does not claim its settlers overseas as Indian citizens but it does expect men and women of Indian origin in other parts of the world to be accorded the fair and equitable treatment it tries to give its own ethnic minorities. The inferior position and harsh treatment of Indians in South Africa was for long supposed to be due to the peculiar arrogance and oppression practised by the white man. But the treatment of the Indian minorities in Ceylon and Burma—countries wherein their disabilities vis-à-vis the indigenous communities are perhaps most acute—raises some doubt as to whether the whole explanation is to be found in terms of race and colour. In the case of these two countries, Asians are prescribing the terms on which other Asians shall live in their midst. Moreover, there are signs that in the new sovereign independent states of Africa, Indians and other Asians will find themselves at a disadvantage compared with the indigenous inhabitants. They came into these places as the camp-followers of the British. Now that the latter are departed, they are, by an irony of fate, regarded as a relic of the selfsame colonialism against which the Indian nationalist movement fought.

The question arises as to whether there is anything practical which Indian foreign policy might have done to replace the arbitrary protection provided by the British Raj for all its subjects with new and solid guarantees for the rights of Indian minorities in other countries. The answer would seem to be that little could, and can, be done save by way of exhortation and example. Of this there has been no lack since independence. On one occasion some years ago, the present writer heard Nehru's address to a delegation of Indians from overseas which had come to represent its sponsors' grievances to him. He spoke to them in the Library of Parliament in New Delhi. 'The most practical advice I can give you', he said, 'is to be good citizens of the country in which you live.' There is very little that an outsider can add.

7

CHINA AND THE BORDER STATES

A SINGLE ISSUE of *The Times* in 1965 had the following headlines in close juxtaposition: *Persecution of Tibetans by Chinese
Occupation Army; Mr Shastri Meets King of Bhutan; Military Build
Up in Ladakh; Russian Military Aid to Nepal.*[1] The newly acquired
importance of the Himalayan border states does not derive
simply from the fact that modern communications have brought
these remote principalities closer to the main stream of world
events; they are in the news because they occupy a strategic
position between India and China, each of which aspires to
something like the role of protecting power or—if that is not
practicable—of guide, philosopher and friend. None of the
Himalayan states can stand by itself: a fact which has provided
a recurring temptation to China to meddle in their affairs, and
gave Britain during the long period of its rule in India a reason
for extending its authority to the point where it claimed the
right to supervise the external relations of these border kingdoms. It is primarily as parties in the Sino-Indian border
dispute that they claim our attention here.

First of all, however, we must look at the circumstances which
led to the war with China in 1962. India and China have a
common frontier running along some 2,000 miles of the great
Himalayan watershed. In the north, Kashmir adjoins the
Chinese province of Sinkiang, but most of the Sino-Indian
frontier lies between India and Tibet, which the Peking
government also claims as a Chinese province and over which
it asserted its jurisdiction with brutal violence in the winter of
1950. For convenience we may adopt Alastair Lamb's categori-

isation[2] and divide the frontier into three sectors: the western sector, which is the boundary between Kashmir, Sinkiang and Tibet and includes the Aksai Chin across which the Chinese have built a motor road linking western Tibet with Sinkiang; the shorter middle sector, about 400 miles in length, which runs along the crest of the Himalayas from the Sutlej to the border of Nepal; and the eastern sector, claimed by India to be the McMahon Line, following the contour of the Assam Himalayas between Bhutan and Burma. This third sector is rather more than 700 miles long and is known as the North East Frontier Agency (NEFA). The Chinese contest the validity of the McMahon Line and therefore of India's claim to the NEFA territory. On a frontier of 2,000 miles in length, situated on the roof of the world, there is ample scope for disagreements. Such a frontier can function satisfactorily as a boundary only if both sides are willing to make it do so.

It would involve too long a digression to trace the historical origins of the dispute, for these reach far into the dim past.* Indeed, the difficulty is to find what is a suitable starting point for any discussion of this highly complicated matter. However, as the Chinese government's first claim over extensive areas on India's side of the border was made on September 8, 1959, we can take this date as marking the point at which Peking threw off the mask of friendship and began seriously to plan frontier incursions. Up to then it had been supposed that, despite Chinese operations over the frontier, the large claims shown on old Chinese maps were errors awaiting revision. Events were soon to show how mistaken this assumption was.

Indian policy regarding its frontier with China rests upon two main principles:

1. The entire length of the frontier (including the borders of Sikkim and Bhutan for which India is responsible) follows natural features, and has either been defined by treaty, or recognised by custom or both.

2. Until the present dispute, no Chinese government has ever protested against the exercise of jurisdiction by the Indian government up to the customary border.

* For instance, one of the documents cited by the Chinese relevant to the dispute is an agreement between Tibet and the former kings of Ladakh dated 1683.

In October 1954, Nehru visited Peking as part of the policy of reviving the 'age-long friendship' which was (mistakenly) supposed to have existed between India and China before its interruption during the British occupation of India. There is no evidence for the existence of this idyllic amity. On the other hand, it is certainly true that the British authorities kept China at a distance during the long period when they were responsible for the security of India's frontiers.

It has been shown that Pandit Nehru enjoyed a near-monopoly in the field of Indian foreign policy, and nowhere was this more marked than in his country's relations with China. That the two chief states of the Asian mainland—both newly free of foreign influence—should draw closer together after the second world war was to be expected. Their leaders were naturally anxious to meet, to exchange greetings and to take the measure of one another. This apart, there was the theory of the ancient friendship between India and China, which was put about without a shred of supporting evidence, in satisfaction of which something had to be done in the way of establishing a close relationship with China. Non-alignment also demanded that India should pay its proper respects to the great Asian Communist power. All these, and a dozen lesser factors, indicated that a special effort should be made to understand the Chinese mind, particularly as Peking was not allowed by the USA to explain itself at the United Nations.

By the time the People's Republic of China had been consolidated in 1949 on the basis of a Marxist-Leninist-Maoist ideology, the Chinese Communist Party had established its authority over the whole of China with the exception of Taiwan (Formosa) and Tibet, both of which remained to be 'liberated'. Any ambitions the Chinese Communists may have had in respect to Taiwan were quickly nipped in the bud by the interposition of the United States Seventh Fleet between the island and the mainland. The Chinese Communist government, having begun preparations at the end of 1949, accordingly decided that the invasion must be postponed *sine die*. But Tibet was another matter entirely; here was no Seventh Fleet to fear, and America was either unable or unwilling to call China to order. Tibet was remote and landlocked. Also it would not be difficult to manufacture a plausible, semi-juridical argument to justify intervention in Tibet which, at intervals in Chinese history, had paid tribute to Peking—albeit under protest. Accordingly, on January 1, 1950, Mao Tse-tung declared the liberation of three million Tibetans from 'imperialist aggression' to be a priority objective of the 'Chinese Peoples' Liberation Army', and the following October Chinese troops entered Tibet to carry out their civilising mission. The Tibetan army—almost medieval in training and equipment—fought bravely but was no match for the better trained Chinese forces. In May 1951 Tibetan representatives went to Peking and there signed a seventeen-point agreement providing for Chinese rule over Tibet, but guaranteeing the continuance of Buddhist institutions, the autonomy of the Tibetan government and the status of the Dalai Lama.

That agreement served for some years to give China's mastery over Tibet some kind of basis in law, though the spirit of the agreement was broken many times. The world conscience was vaguely troubled that a small, weak nation, which asked nothing more than to be left to enjoy its backwardness in peace, should be brought under a ruthless new Asian despotism. But what could be done about it? What help could be given? India was Tibet's closest neighbour, or so it seemed to the majority of people whose knowledge of the Himalayas is somewhat patchy. Would India not do something about it? Certainly, Nehru, who had acquiesced in the 1951 agreement, soon began to have some reservations about the way the Chinese had resumed their overlordship of Tibet. But, though it is easy enough to say that Nehru and India should have done something, for all practical purposes Lhasa was as remote from Delhi as from Whitehall.

In 1959 the Tibetans revolted and the Dalai Lama, who was greatly revered by Buddhists all over the world, fled to India. It was not the first time a Dalai Lama had escaped southwards before advancing Chinese forces. It had happened in 1910, but a year later the Manchus were overthrown in China and the then Dalai Lama returned to Lhasa, from which all Chinese troops and representatives were promptly expelled and sent back to China. In 1959, however, the Tibetans had a more determined Chinese administration to deal with and,

though their guerrillas continued to put up a stubborn resistance in the Khampa areas, the revolt in Lhasa itself was fairly
quickly put down. After an adventurous journey, partly on
foot and always in disguise, the young Dalai Lama arrived on
Indian soil at Tawang in the North East Frontier Agency.
There he was met by, amongst others, representatives of the
world press, particularly of British and American newspapers,
who had been waiting for days to meet him. His simple and
unaffected but dignified bearing appealed to them at once. In
the modern idiom he 'made the headlines' immediately and in a
big way. India committed the mortal sin—in Chinese eyes—of
welcoming him and of giving him asylum at Mussoorie. He had
considerable spiritual prestige all over Asia, and that he should
have chosen free India in preference to totalitarian China was
not without its moral for the smaller countries of the region.
The present writer believes that this was a main factor in
determining Peking's subsequent policy towards India.

But here we must turn back a little. In December 1956 Chou
En-lai had visited Delhi. The Indians claim that in private
talks with Nehru he indicated China's readiness to recognise the
McMahon Line as the frontier with India. In October 1957 the
Chinese announced the completion of the Yehcheng-Gartok
road, better known as the Sinkiang-Tibet highway; but they
did not disclose the route, thereby quite naturally arousing
Indian suspicions. The Chinese had, in fact, constructed a
motor road which traversed territory which was assumed in
Delhi to have been part of the Ladakh region of India for
centuries and the frontiers of which had been accepted by
China in a treaty of 1842. In November 1958 the first serious
frontier incident occurred: the Chinese government notified
India that an Indian patrol, reported missing since the end of
August, had been detained on 'the Sinkiang-Tibet road on
Chinese territory' and had been 'deported' through the
Karakoram Pass. At about the same time, India officially
complained that Chinese maps were showing as Chinese large
areas of India's North East Frontier Agency and of eastern
Ladakh, some Indian areas in the central sector of the frontier
and parts of Bhutan. In explanation Chou En-lai said this
derived from maps published in China before the 'liberation',

and that China believed 'a new way of drawing the boundary' would eventually result from surveys and 'consultation with various neighbouring countries'.

By now it was becoming clear to Nehru that it was deliberate Chinese policy to try to confuse the issue as much as possible and to drag the small, and poorly documented, frontier states into the dispute. His reply was terse and to the point: the original excuse given for major irregularities in the maps—namely Chinese preoccupation with other matters—had lost its force after nine years of Communist rule. 'There can be no question', he said, 'of these large parts of India being anything but Indian, and there is no dispute about them.' From this point onwards, relations between the two countries deteriorated rapidly. In the summer of 1959 the Dalai Lama was described in an official Peking Note as a Chinese rebel who had been abducted to India—which would seem to most people to be a contradiction in terms. In the same Note, India was invited to recognise the United States as China's main enemy and, as a sign of friendship for China, to abandon 'two fronts'. Thus China made a bid to wean India away from a policy of non-alignment, which the present writer regards as another of the major reasons for China's hostility to India. In any case, as a practical matter, India's recognition of Sino-American enmity can have little relevance to the facts of the frontier dispute. This is politics at the level of the school playground.

By September 1959 the Chinese had officially enlarged their claim to something like 40,000 square miles of Indian territory in the western, central and eastern sectors of the frontier. It was now certain that the Chinese Communists were out to make serious trouble if they did not get their way, though the sheer effrontery of their demands was such as to prejudice their case from the beginning. At the back of these large territorial claims on India hover the imperial pretensions of the past, which China's conversion to Communism seems in no way to have allayed. Peking alleged that the frontier, as understood by India, was a 'problem left over from history', and demanded that it should be open to renegotiation in its entirety; but they cited history only where it appeared to support their claims, rejecting as 'imperialist' those documents which did not. This was the unpromising negotiation position which had been

reached by the end of 1959, by which time frontier incidents
were assuming a more sanguinary character and the language
of the notes and verbal communications between the two
governments was becoming increasingly grave. At the end of
the year, on December 26, the Chinese showed their hand:
the Indian ambassador in Peking was handed a Note rejecting
Indian interpretations of treaties and tradition as they affected
most of the points in dispute, and insisting that the entire
Sino-Indian frontier had 'never been delimited and is therefore yet to be settled through negotiations'. In effect, China
claimed an option to raise a dispute at any point along its
2,000 mile frontier with India.

A claim to delimit afresh all or any part of the Sino-Indian
frontier meant the complete rejection, among other things, of
the McMahon Line, which was the hinge on which turned all
agreements between India, Burma and Tibet on the frontier
east of Bhutan. The McMahon Line (named after the chief
British-Indian delegate) dates from the time of the Simla
Conference of 1913–14 between India, Tibet and China. It was
in no sense, as the Chinese have since suggested, a new frontier
drawn by 'aggressive imperialism'. Indeed, its chief merit is
that it is largely a natural frontier, running mostly along the
crest of the Himalayan range. The McMahon Line, as drawn
on the map attached to the Simla Convention, was never
challenged by the Chinese representative at that time or
afterwards. His signature was later repudiated by the Chinese
government, but this was in protest against the internal
boundary between Outer and Inner Tibet and Inner Tibet and
China. There was no protest over the McMahon Line as the
frontier of India, and in the Sino-Burmese boundary agreement of 1960 the Chinese recognised the McMahon Line as
their frontier with Burma which, at the time of the Simla
Conference, had been part of British India. Thus its suitability
as a physical frontier was never in question; more objection-
able were its political implications, for in Chinese eyes they
appeared to recognise the independence and sovereignty of
Tibet.

It is not proposed to follow in detail the long and tortuous
course of Sino-Indian diplomacy, or the exchange of Notes and

other communications. These can be studied elsewhere*, but some mention must be made of the final stages which led up to the conflict in the autumn of 1962. In April 1960 the two premiers, Nehru and Chou En-lai, met for five days in Delhi but failed to resolve their differences, which is hardly surprising as these had been hardening steadily during the previous five years. They did, however, agree that there should be meetings of officials to examine documents and prepare a joint report and that every effort should be made to avoid friction in the border areas. The examinations of documentary material took place in Rangoon, and a joint report was published by Delhi (but not by Peking) in February 1961. In December 1961 the Chinese proposed negotiating a new agreement 'in accordance with the Five Principles' to replace the Sino-Indian Treaty on Trade and Intercourse with Tibet, when this expired in June 1962. India replied that the first essential for starting such negotiations was 'the reversal of aggressive policies' and 'the restoration of a climate which assures strict observance of the Five Principles both in the letter and the spirit'. In May 1962 Peking announced an agreement with Pakistan 'to locate and align their common frontier'. Throughout the summer, events were gathering momentum and, though neither the Indian people nor some of their legislators knew it, the situation was rapidly moving towards a crisis.

For the rest of the year, and until the actual invasion of India took place, there were charges and counter-charges of intrusion, clashes between border patrols, the setting up of new and disputed check posts, and all the usual accompaniments of frontier tension. Typical of the many protests is one of June 1962 in which India cites 'carefully verified reports' from Ladakh that 'Chinese troops are daily intruding into Indian territory, pushing forward on trucks and jeeps, blasting the mountainside with heavy explosives, constructing new military bases and extending bases already set up'. And it does seem indisputable that the Chinese were assiduously preparing for the invasion that was to come. A month later an Indian Note was giving co-ordinates and particulars of nine new Chinese posts inside Ladakh, 'poised in menacing proximity to existing

* See e.g. the several chronological records published by the Information Department of the Government of India.

Indian posts in the area'. Throughout September and most of October hardly a day passed without allegations of some kind being made by one side or the other, while an increasingly threatening tone pervaded the Chinese communications. China repeatedly offered negotiations, but stipulated that there were to be no preconditions. To the uncommitted states of Asia and Africa, this might seem a very reasonable starting point for talks; but acceptance meant that India would throw away the whole of its bargaining position before sitting down at the conference table. As befits any self-respecting country with an elected government, India insisted that the Chinese should desist from their intrusions south of the McMahon Line as a preliminary to discussions for the revision of the frontier.

On October 12, 1962, Pandit Nehru announced that the Indian army had been given instructions to push the Chinese back across the McMahon Line where they had violated it. The following day China announced that 'the Indian aggressors must bear full responsibility for their crimes', but Delhi declined to negotiate further under duress and the kind of blackmail to which they had now been subjected for several years. A week later, at dawn on October 20, the Chinese launched a full scale invasion at strategic points along the McMahon Line, at the same time assuming the offensive in Ladakh. There was no declaration of war, but the Indian chargé d'affaires in Peking was handed a note alleging 'frenzied attacks' by Indian troops and a refusal to negotiate.

By now, both sides had crossed their respective Rubicons and were too deeply committed for negotiations to have any chance of success. The world accordingly witnessed the spectacle of one Asian power committing aggression against another— something it had been assured could never happen. The first Indian communiqués provided no cheer and reported Indian troops falling back with heavy losses in the Tawang area of NEFA. Soon it became clear that on both the Ladakh and eastern sectors the Indians were going to be hard pressed to find and hold a defensible line. They had not been trained to operate at heights of between 15,000 and 20,000 feet above sea level. Nehru told the country to prepare itself for a long war and President Radakrishnan declared a state of national emergency. India had been taken by surprise by the suddenness and ferocity of the Chinese attack. Its troops fought gallantly, and there were many instances of individual heroism. There was a great upsurge of national pride and patriotism amongst the civil population. But this was not enough to hold back a ruthless, well trained and better equipped invader. By the end of October Indian troops had been dispossessed of the road-head of Tawang (strategically, one of the most important places in the NEFA territory), and after a short pause other Chinese attacks were launched along the whole northern border, stretching from a point within fifteen miles of Burmese territory in the east to Ladakh at the western end of the frontier. It was estimated that by early November between 2,000 and 2,500 Indians had been killed. Chinese losses were also reported to be considerable, but this was not subsequently confirmed.

By the middle of November Ladakh was virtually lost to India, while the Chinese had firmly established themselves inside the North East Frontier Agency. A week later the Chinese were within miles of Tezpur, an important district headquarters town in Assam. Their capture of Walong, further to the east, had opened the road to the oilfields of Digboi, and many observers considered it well within the bounds of possibility that the whole of Assam, north of the Brahmaputra as well as the oilfields south of the river, could be occupied for the asking. Then there came a dramatic and totally unexpected move. On November 21 the Chinese announced a cease-fire; they declared their intention to begin a withdrawal on December 1 to positions in NEFA twenty kilometres behind the actual line of control which existed in November 1959, and in Ladakh to a similar distance behind the actual line of control as it existed in November 1962. The Peking government's statement was first announced through the medium of the New China News Agency and confirmed a day or two later by the receipt of the official text in New Delhi. The Chinese withdrawal soon began, and though the Indian government avoided having to acknowledge the cease-fire terms officially, in fact it accepted them. Indeed, it could hardly do otherwise. After the calamitous series of defeats which it had sustained, the Indian army was no longer an integrated fighting force but a number of pockets of resistance of varying degrees of strength. The political background to this humiliating defeat is discussed below. At the purely military level, it can be ascribed to defective intelligence, at least regarding the eastern front, inexperienced generalship, and widespread unpreparedness to meet a better equipped enemy in the type of climatic and other conditions to be found in the Himalayas from the foothills upwards. Indian losses amounted to 3,080 killed, with large numbers of wounded and missing.

India's self-confidence was badly shaken and the Chinese did not spare its feelings. Warning Delhi of the consequences of any breach in the cease-fire terms, the Chinese Note of November 21 said:

> The Chinese Government solemnly declares that . . . it reserves the right to strike back in self-defence and the Indian Government will be held completely responsible for all the grave consequences arising therefrom. The people of the world will then see even more clearly who is peace-loving and who is bellicose; who upholds friendship between the Chinese and Indian peoples and Asian-African solidarity and who is undermining them; who is protecting the common interests of Asian and African peoples in their struggle against imperialism and colonialism and who is violating and damaging these common interests.

Before examining the effects of this disastrous affair on Nehru and his government, we should try to state more precisely what were China's motives in launching a bloody and unnecessary war against India. Unnecessary, because Peking could have secured what might properly be judged to belong to China by peaceful means such as arbitration by the International Court at the Hague, which at one stage Nehru offered. Opinions as to why China launched its offensive when it did will differ for a long time to come, but this writer believes the following to have been important influences in the decision to attack India: 1. Resentment at the generally sympathetic Indian attitude to Tibet and the Dalai Lama. 2. A doctrinaire communist belief that the McMahon Line was foisted on China by Britain and a determination to rectify matters. 3. Having built a road across Ladakh by stealth, it became settled policy for China to occupy the area permanently. 4. To demonstrate to Asia, and particularly to the Himalayan border states, the military prowess of

China and reinforce its claim to be the dominant power in the region. And 5—more doubtfully—to dislocate the Indian economy, thus making sure that no democratic eastern nation might progress as rapidly as Communist China. A friend of the writer, who was one of the very few English businessmen allowed to reside in China throughout this or any other period of communist rule, reports that the frontier war aroused remarkably little general interest and that, considering the scale of the operations, the newspapers did not have much to say about it. It is difficult to explain this apparent indifference, but it may well be that to a nation of more than 600 million people, the killing of a mere 3,000 represents nothing more than a frontier skirmish.

But, however the affair fits into the puzzle of Chinese politics, it had quite considerable repercussions in India and upon Nehru personally. Rightly or wrongly, Krishna Menon was held to be a central figure in the army's defeat. He had been appointed India's minister of Defence in April 1957, and had thus been in office five and a half years when the invasion occurred. Apart from being defence minister, he exercised an informal, but considerable, influence in the sphere of foreign affairs which, unlike his other cabinet colleagues, he could discuss on level terms with the prime minister, who was said to consult him freely. Krishna Menon had also led the Indian delegation at the United Nations and had been an effective spokesman for his country on the perennial subject of Kashmir. He certainly was a close personal friend and confidant of Nehru's as well as the chief advocate of a too-trusting acceptance of China's promises. It is known that he certainly stands well to the left in politics, is a skilful negotiator and something of a lone wolf in Indian public life, to whom Nehru had a curious and (to many Indians) inexplicable attachment. Thus, by the weight of evidence that was inevitably somewhat conjectural, he was automatically cast for the role of *éminence grise*.

The indictment against Menon was lengthy and we need not attempt to itemise every detail. His tenure of the Defence Ministry covered the period of mounting tension with China, and the vast majority of Indians considered that he had not been

sufficiently alert to the direction in which events were rapidly
moving. Political promotions had deprived the army of some
of its best leaders. That apart, the army was quite unequipped
to give battle at the high altitudes of the Himalayas; no amount
of personal bravery could make good the basic shortages of
creature necessities for mountain warfare. The poor showing
made by the Indian army resulted in a demand for Menon's
resignation by the parliamentary Congress Party supported
by the president. Nehru is understood to have shown the
utmost reluctance to get rid of his colleague and to have
fought stubbornly to retain him. But the weight of public
opinion was too much, even for the prime minister, and
Krishna Menon had to go.

Yet although the dismissed minister of Defence must bear a
heavy share of the responsibility for the catastrophe, some of
the blame undoubtedly belongs to the prime minister for his
apparent complacency, his misreading of a situation on the
border that was becoming more dangerous every day, and for
the failure to ensure that adequate preparations for the defence
of the country were put in hand. Lack of realism, rather than
neutralism, had brought India to the very brink of disaster;
and though the Indian people were prepared to forgive Pandit
Nehru, as their favourite son, almost anything, it is doubtful if,
in the remaining seventeen months of his life, he ever quite
regained his ascendancy over parliament and the country.
He had by now become a visibly ailing man who moved
slowly and with care to his place in the Lok Sabha. There was a
distant look in his eyes, as though he remembered the words of
his master, Mahatma Gandhi, who spoke of embracing death
as 'the incomparable friend'.

The abrupt termination of the fighting, the shifty, inconclusive
and unsatisfactory character of Peking's terms for peace,
strengthen the impression that China's action was intended,
inter alia, as a demonstration of strength from which the border
states should draw the appropriate inferences. After exchanges
designed to clarify the Chinese proposals, Nehru described them
in his reply to Chou En-lai as 'a definite attempt to retain under
cover of preliminary cease-fire arrangements physical possession over the area which China claims and to secure which the

massive attack since October 20, 1962 was mounted by your forces'. In contrast, he declared that the Indian proposal for a return to the *status quo* of September 8, 1962, was a clear and straightforward proposition. India had not in any way impeded the Chinese cease-fire and withdrawal, and he reiterated that it was in favour of disengagement by agreement. But the line to be observed had first to be determined. However, agreement on this point was as far away as ever and India was in no position to enforce its will.

India had, nonetheless, managed to salvage something from the wreck; it had the advantages of the cease-fire without formally recognising its terms, and had succeeded in keeping open its claims to the territory which the Chinese had over-run. Meanwhile, various friends had been active on India's behalf. American and British political and military missions arrived in Delhi in the third week of November 1962 and began a series of discussions about the military aid needed to bring India's defences up to strength. This is essentially a long-term affair and much of it is secret. A little later, in the middle of December, a conference of non-aligned nations was called in Colombo. Cambodia, Ceylon, Burma, Indonesia, the United Arab Republic and Ghana sent representatives. By the end of the month proposals for peace were drafted, and Mrs Bandaranaike, prime minister of Ceylon, went to Peking to present them on behalf of what came to be called the Colombo Conference of Non-Aligned States. She was ceremoniously received by Chou En-lai, who carefully placed the document in the appropriate pigeon-hole—where it has lain ever since. The 'Colombo Proposals' were well intentioned, but—like the *Panch Shila*—have been forgotten except by a handful of connoisseurs of the minutiae of diplomacy.

But, as everyone with experience of the East knows, once the Chinese have got their foot in a particular door they are not easily dislodged. At a moment which was crucial for India in the 1965 fighting with Pakistan, they delivered an ultimatum (dated September 17) demanding that all military installations on or over the China-Sikkim boundary be dismantled within three days (subsequently extended to six), or India must face consequences which would be 'grave'. The matter is discussed in more detail elsewhere in this book; but the manner and timing of China's demands make it obvious that its emnity towards India is not likely to disappear quickly.

The Himalayan States

Nepal

Of the three border kingdoms of Nepal, Sikkim and Bhutan, the first named is, militarily and otherwise, the most important, though Sikkim has a high strategic rating in relation to the Sino-Indian struggle for control of the Himalayan border. Following the Anglo-Nepalese war of 1814-16, Nepal entered the orbit of British influence and in fact became, by treaty, a British protected state which enjoyed a very substantial degree of autonomy. In the pre-independence period, right up to 1947, the Indian National Congress Party was most punctilious in paying its respect to the maharajah on his annual cold-weather visit to Calcutta, for it regarded Nepal as the only independent Hindu kingdom at that time.* According to General Tuker:†

> Nepal, as the British left her in 1947, was the independent Kingdom of the Gurkhas, a slab of land five hundred and twenty miles long by some hundred broad from Sikkim to the Kali River, its boundary with Kumaon. It marches with Tibet along the lower mountains. . . . Always they have been a sovereign and independent people so far as the British have been concerned. Why they should have treated us (so faithfully) is something of a mystery. . . . A small warlike people who, in defence of their own independence,

* To avoid confusion, it should be noted that, until recent years, the maharajah was the hereditary prime minister. The king of Nepal was a spiritual and religious head of state, effective power being vested in the maharajah. With the active encouragement of Nehru, a constitutional monarchy was proclaimed in 1951, and the king became the real head of government, operating through a council of ministers.

† General Tuker served in India for thirty-four years, the whole of his regimental service being with the Brigade of Gurkhas. His knowledge and understanding of the men of Nepal is based on much active service with them —in Mesopotamia and Persia in the 1914–18 war, on the North-West Frontier of India in the 1930s, and in North Africa, Italy, and Burma in the second world war.

have for two centuries shielded India from the swelling power of Tartaric Asia.[3]

For over a hundred years Nepal regarded Britain as its chief ally, and as long as Britain was strong in Asia through its Indian establishment and China was weak (as was the case from the mid-nineteenth century), this was a sensible view of the outside world as seen from Khatmandu. But the withdrawal of Britain from South Asia and the revival of Chinese power in Tibet in 1960 changed the picture completely; Nepal's role was again that of the traditional buffer state whose policy it must be to play off India against China and vice-versa. The young King Mahendra, who succeeded his father King Tribhuvana in 1955, decided that this was the part his country was cast for. In 1956 he sent his prime minister, Tanka Prasad Acharya, to Peking where a sweetener had been prepared in the form of a Chinese development loan of $12 million. This was the first of a number of visits and more aid. The Indians were by now thoroughly alarmed, and even more so when a Sino-Nepalese border agreement was signed in 1961. But the Nepal government was distinctly embarrassed when the Chinese offered it a defence pact in the event of aggression: a gesture which came at a moment when dissident Nepalese politicians were raiding the country from bases in Uttar Pradesh and Bihar in India in an attempt to overthrow the king's administration. Nepal had no desire to become a bone of contention between its two powerful neighbours. India soon began to realise that an ancient friendship, or the special relationship it claimed, was breaking up; from that moment the Indian government strove genuinely—but sometimes mistakenly —to put things on a better footing, for which purpose it had considerable natural advantages. Over 95 per cent of Nepal's trade is with India, which supplies nearly all the manufactures Nepal consumes and which receives most of its exports—the chief of which is manpower. The men of Nepal still go into the British and Indian armies, and indeed are reckoned amongst the bravest and most capable of their fighting troops. Their remittances home, and those of the growing numbers of Nepalis now in civil employment in eastern India, are the principal element in Nepal's balance of payments.

E

It was perhaps inevitable, but nonetheless unfortunate, that India should have become involved in the three-cornered struggles among the royal house and Rana family, hereditary holders of the office of prime minister, and the leftwing Nepali Congress politicians. As early as 1950 Pandit Nehru stated India's position very clearly to parliament, when he declared it was the intention 'not only to continue the old friendship with Nepal, but to put it on a firmer base'. Then, in measured words, he added: 'In common with others our Ambassador naturally went to the King as the head of State, although during the last hundred years or so the King has had no say in his Government. We continue to recognise the King. We see no reason why we should do anything else. We propose to continue to recognise the King.' And a few days later he said: 'As the House is aware we have observed the strictest neutrality in the internal struggle in Nepal.' Neutral perhaps; but India could not be indifferent to what was going on in Nepal, and watched with increasing uneasiness the struggle which ultimately led to the downfall of the Ranas. Indeed, to the extent that the Indian government advised King Tribhuvana on the type of constitution and limited representative government that Nepal might adopt when the Ranas eventually disappeared, Delhi may be said to have had a hand in the making of the new regime in Nepal.

Officially Nepal's policy towards India is one of neutralism, though during the course of another of his 1950 parliamentary utterances Pandit Nehru said: 'No other country can have as intimate a relationship with Nepal as ours. We would like every other country to appreciate the intimate geographical and cultural relationship that exists between India and Nepal.' But during the 1950s and 1960s, India was caught in the not unfamiliar but painful posture of wishing to back two political horses that were running in competition, i.e. trying to demonstrate its sympathy towards an allegedly democratic organisation in the shape of the Nepali Congress, and at the same time do business with the authoritarian regime to which the Congress was bitterly opposed. India, indeed, remained passive while the banned Nepali Congress carried on its dubious activities from the Indian side of the border. But inside Nepal itself the people, hitherto largely indifferent to the Nepali Congress, rallied with surprising effect to the side of the king, who had for some time been rethinking his external policies.

As a result of these second thoughts, not only did the king accept Chinese aid but he also agreed to the construction of a road between Lhasa and Khatmandu, which is now expected to be completed in 1966. Agreements with Pakistan were signed in December 1962 and again in February 1963 which give Nepal the use of facilities at the port of Chittagong in East Pakistan (as an alternative to Calcutta), and which provide for barter in commodities that are also traded with India. A road in southern Nepal is also projected; this will obviate the transhipment of goods, destined from one point in Nepal to another, through Indian territory. All these measures were designed to reduce Nepal's dependence on India and to give the country more elbow-room. Between November 1951 and May 1959, Nepal had nine governments appointed by the king, and the game of musical chairs has continued at intervals ever since. In the latter month, a Nepali Congress administration was formed, led by that ruthless Marxist, B. P. Koirala, with a programme of socialism not unlike that of the Indian Congress Party. Early in 1960, Koirala was in Peking where he negotiated a $20 million grant. The drift towards Communist China was unmistakable. The irony is that both India and the United States are understood to have financed the Nepali Congress Party.[4]

In August 1963, the king paid a state visit to India. The lessons both countries had learnt from the Chinese border attack of the previous autumn pointed strongly to the mutual need which India and Nepal had for one another. A steady improvement in Indo-Nepalese relations began which has continued to the present, though it is doubtful if India will ever again enjoy a monopoly of Nepal's favours. Since he has taken over the reins of government, King Mahendra has used his council of ministers purely as an administrative body; in fact, they are little more than a façade and all decisions of state must have the king's personal approval. The royal assent is now an indispensable part of the constitution of Nepal, which in a few short and dramatic years has rid itself of the despotism by which it was governed for more than a century, while at the same time rejecting the rule of a clique of disparate and quarrelsome politicians, mostly of a strong leftwing persuasion. As long as the king commands the loyalty of the army, he will continue to govern the country. This is a prime condition of his authority. Even so, of the political parties now banned, the communists are the strongest.

Some time has been spent on the internal affairs of Nepal because they illustrate the kind of situation in which Nehru was prone to take the rather simple view that, if only you removed the wicked tyrant the people would manage their affairs, big and small, by peaceful discussion and agreement. He had the Greek philosopher's love of reason and moderation: the Nepalese situation called for the shrewdness and realism of a Machiavelli. In this respect Nehru is to be seen as a true descendant of nineteenth-century liberalism, differing greatly from the modern political boss who thrives in the Afro-Asian world today and in certain parts of the western hemisphere. If his career be examined closely, this streak of ingenuousness and other-worldliness can be detected from time to time. It must frequently have exasperated his advisers.

Bhutan

Bhutan and Sikkim are two little-known Himalayan states, which today possess for India a strategic significance that is in inverse proportion to their size and importance. Of the two, Bhutan is much the larger, lying at the eastern end of the Himalayan range and slightly to the north-west of the Brahmaputra valley. It is bordered on the north and east by Tibet and India, on the west by Sikkim and on the south by India. Its length from east to west is 190 miles and at its broadest it is 90 miles across. Bhutan's population is thought to be about 700,000, of whom about 600,000 live in or near the capital which is called Punakha. It thus conforms in every respect to the classic pattern of the buffer state. A good understanding between India and Bhutan is desirable because of the submontane passes which lead from one to the other, and of which at least one would provide a usable invasion route for a land force attacking India.

Relations between the two countries have been regulated by a series of agreements beginning with a treaty with the East

India Company in 1744. In the 1865 treaty with the government of British India, the Bhutan government was given a subsidy of fifty thousand rupees a year; in 1910 the amount was increased to Rs 1 lakh and in 1942 was further increased to Rs 2 lakhs. The British-Indian government of the day undertook to exercise no interference in the internal affairs of Bhutan, in return for which Bhutan promised to be guided by Delhi in all matters pertaining to external relations. At the time of independence in 1947, Bhutan was theoretically and legally a sovereign independent state, and the successor government in India hastened to conclude a fresh treaty in supersession of all previous documents. The subsidy was increased to Rs 5 lakhs annually and the provision governing external affairs was continued. If account is taken of Bhutan's substantial trade with India and of the aid it is offered, it is clear that it does fairly well out of the connection with its larger and more sophisticated southern neighbour.

But it is difficult for an almost totally illiterate population to make the fullest use of aid, especially when its government forbids the entry of foreigners into the country. This royal edict serves to keep out infiltrating Nepalese, of whom the Bhutanese are both suspicious and resentful. Contrary to his usual philosophy, when Nehru visited Punakha in 1958 he advised the Bhutanese to persist in their policy of exclusion, and this may well have been contributory to the later misunderstandings between India and Nepal. Four-fifths of the population of Bhutan are of Tibetan stock and they speak a language related to the Tibetan tongue. They are Buddhists and acknowledge the Dalai Lama as their spiritual guide. Their natural affiliations are thus with Tibet rather than with India or China.

Nehru paid his visit to Bhutan in 1958 largely because the Indian point of view on events in Tibet required some explanation. The following year, in 1959, the Bhutanese prime minister went to New Delhi to seek assurances about his country's defence. There is no formal defence treaty between the two states, though India has declared that an attack on Bhutan by China would be considered as an act of aggression against India itself. This was before the frontier war of 1962, and presumably the assurance still holds good. On April 5, 1964 Jigme Dorji,

prime minister of Bhutan, was assassinated. The dead administrator was a friend of India, with which he favoured close ties.
His demise was the high point of some months of political un-
rest unusual for Bhutan; but there is nothing concrete to
connect the killing with the Chinese. In January 1965 the king
of Bhutan visited Calcutta and had talks with Lal Bahadur
Shastri. Pledges of friendship were renewed, and the king
expressed a wish that his country (already a member of the
Colombo Plan) should join the United Nations. He considered
that this would strengthen Bhutan's position, precariously
situated as it is as a buffer zone between India and China, and
give it greater freedom to accept aid from the West. Thus,
after centuries of isolation in the damp mists of the Himalayas,
Bhutan seeks to take a small, but not unimportant, part in
world affairs, and to join the community of nations. In spite of
Nehru's earlier caution over the admission of foreigners to
Bhutan, it is very probable that this new development would
have commanded his support.

Sikkim

Sandwiched between Nepal and Bhutan is the tiny mountain
kingdom of Sikkim, about 3,000 square miles in area and with a
mixed population of Bhutias, Lepchas and Nepalis numbering
about 150,000. The ruling family are Lepchas, the original
inhabitants, but now numbering no more than about fifteen
per cent of the total population. For India, Sikkim has enormous
strategic importance as it represents a narrow defile through
the Himalayas to Assam and the Brahmaputra valley. India's
influence on the administration is of a much more direct kind
than in the case of Nepal and Bhutan. There is an Indian
diplomatic representative at the Sikkimese capital, Gangtok,
and the *dewan* (or chief adviser) of the maharajah of Sikkim
is appointed from the ranks of the Indian Administrative
Service. India also maintains important roads in Sikkim,
including the two main caravan routes to Tibet; along these
travels news of the outside world, of which Sikkim has always
been more aware than Bhutan. Under the influence of India
the revenue and land tenure systems, previously crude and
harsh, have been reformed, and as a result the peasants are

somewhat better off. But in the most general terms, Sikkim's problem is to preserve its own identity; this means to resist gradual absorption by the more progressive Nepalese, who already constitute more than half the population; to accept as much Indianisation as is necessary, but no more; and to withstand the pressure of Communism from the north. Obviously its own resources are quite inadequate to all or any of these three tasks, and the signs are that Sikkim will continue to look to India for assistance and advice. That it occupies a position of central importance in Sino-Indian affairs is clear from the fact that, in February 1965, the Indian government found it necessary to send a note to Peking completely denying charges that its troops had built twenty-seven military structures on the Chinese side of the Tibet-Sikkim border.

*   *   *

With the deterioration of India's relations with China from 1959, its dealings with the Himalayan border states took on a new importance. Up to then it had been sufficient to continue (and India had largely been content to do so) the kind of relationship which the former British-India government had with these remote, inaccessible, mountainous and backward countries. In the conditions in which it operated before 1947, this paternalistic link between Delhi and the Himalayan kingdoms served the purpose well enough. It ensured the peace and tranquillity of the area and, if no striking social and economic progress was made, there were likewise no great upheavals. The tempo of life was slow but sure. But the rise of Communism in China introduced an entirely new factor. A resurgent China asserted a supposedly ancient right to suzerainty over Tibet and made territorial claims beyond Tibet's proper borders, which India was bound to reject. It is much to be doubted that India would have been in a better fighting position in 1962 if it had pursued a different policy towards the border states.

It is charged against Nehru that he was too tolerant of Chinese behaviour in Tibet and of the duplicity of Chinese actions on India's northern borders, particularly regarding the road across Ladakh linking Sinkiang and western Tibet. He certainly showed considerable patience, but it is questionable whether earlier action would have deflected the Chinese in their plans or have affected the eventual result of the fighting. The situation was such that nothing would be gained for India by publicly voicing what, for most of the time, were only suspicions. As the head of India's government, Nehru must take some of the blame for the military unpreparedness, though the primary responsibility lies elsewhere.

But here again, a caveat must be entered. Before the Japanese invasion of Assam via Burma in the second world war, the whole of the thinking and planning of the Indian army, controlled by Britain for a hundred years, had been orientated towards the North-West Frontier, which—in addition to its strategic significance—provided a magnificient training ground for troops. So a Briton cannot be too critical if post-independence policy failed to produce in a few short years an army that could fight under entirely different conditions.

For Nehru himself the whole business was a bitter personal disappointment; the Chinese action precipitated a complete breakdown of the kind of system by which he envisaged international disputes might be settled. In the face of much evidence to the contrary, he had continued to believe in *Panch Shila*. But China had rejected the idea of peaceful coexistence, and by the time Nehru died it was clear that the Chinese wanted to create as many Communist states as possible throughout the Afro-Asian world. Above all, China now has the atomic bomb, the possession of which is bound to alter the balance of power in Asia. Events have begun to prove the truth of Nehru's words to the Asian Relations Conference in New Delhi in 1947 when he said: 'In this crisis in world history, Asia will necessarily play a vital role. The countries of Asia can no longer be used as pawns by others; they are bound to have their own policies in world affairs.'

8

THE
COMMONWEALTH

AT THE TIME OF HIS DEATH, Pandit Nehru shared with Sir Robert Menzies, the Australian prime minister, the distinction of being the longest serving premier in the Commonwealth. The various mutations from interim government to republican cabinet make it difficult to put an exact date to the beginning of the Nehru premiership for the purpose of measuring it in precise terms alongside others. But the comparison with Sir Robert Menzies is roughly accurate. Furthermore, Nehru attended every Commonwealth Prime Ministers Conference from 1948 to 1962, visiting London for the purpose practically every year during that period. He became one of the best known Commonwealth statesmen in London and a familiar figure on those occasions when its leaders took counsel together. He believed strongly in the Commonwealth as an idea and as an institution. How came it that a man who spent so much of his life opposing the British should, in the years of his fulfilment, choose for his country membership of that essentially British conception, the Commonwealth, and in fact play a leading part in adapting it to the changed post-war condition of a dissolving empire?

In the days of the freedom struggle, when it was a recognised part of nationalist political in-fighting to decry everything British, it had been assumed in India that Dominion status represented a sort of second-class brand of independence, and the Congress Party pledged itself to the idea of a republic and a complete break with the Commonwealth. However, Nehru at the end of the Premiers Conference in October 1948 declared:

'This meeting has shown me there is great scope for the Commonwealth.' Two months later, at the Jaipur session of the Indian National Congress, in a speech on India's external affairs, he said that membership of the Commonwealth had involved no interference whatever with India's foreign policy. He was obviously preparing the ground for India to continue its membership of this unique institution. And so in April 1949, at a Conference of Commonwealth Prime Ministers specially convened for the purpose, a formula was worked out whereby India, when it became a republic on January 26, 1950, was enabled to remain a member of the Commonwealth. The formula consisted of a simple declaration in which India expressed the desire 'to continue her full membership in the Commonwealth of Nations and her acceptance of the King as symbol of the free association of its independent member nations and as such the Head of the Commonwealth. On their part the governments of the other Commonwealth countries declared that they 'accept and recognise India's continuing membership in accordance with the terms of this declaration'.

But it was not entirely a matter of finding a formula agreeable to the Conference or one which fitted a republic into an organisation that was grounded in an ancient constitutional monarchy. Nehru had also to secure the acceptance of the Commonwealth idea by his own people. Accordingly, on May 16, 1949, he moved the following resolution in the Constituent Assembly, which was then acting as both parliament and constitution-making body: 'Resolved that this Assembly do hereby ratify the declaration agreed to by the Prime Minister of India, on the continued membership of India in the Commonwealth of Nations, as set out in the official statement issued at the conclusion of the Conference of the Commonwealth Prime Ministers in London on April 19, 1949.'

For the framework of this important speech Nehru dissected the four paragraphs of the official statement which had been issued at the end of the London Conference, which had been specially convened for the purpose of dealing with India's application. Membership, he said, represented 'an agreement by free will, to be terminated by free will'. The Commonwealth was not a legal entity with rules and regulations, and, as its head, the Crown had 'status' rather than 'function'. The cast of Nehru's mind was such that he was in his element when dealing with something rather vague and imprecise, and from this point of view Commonwealth membership was an admirable subject for him. He emphasised that if the House approved what he had done and accepted the resolution, no further action by way of law or legislation was necessary. It was on the face of it so simple that some people might be tempted to think there were risks in joining an organisation such as the Commonwealth. He assured his listeners that this was not so. Nehru also dealt with the difficult question of citizenship and rejected the idea of a Commonwealth citizenship of which there had been some talk at about that time. He explained that what he had been searching for was 'something that would advance the cause of India, something that would advance the cause of peace and yet something which would be strictly and absolutely true to every single pledge that we (the Indian people) had taken . . . because no country can make progress by playing fast and loose with the principles which it has declared'. The Commonwealth association seemed to point the way towards these objectives. He ended a long and historic speech with a reference to the 'touch of healing' which was inherent in Commonwealth membership, and told parliament that— though some members wished to move amendments—the resolution for which he sought acceptance was not susceptible of amendment, and must be adopted in its entirety. The motion was carried and the occasion is on the record as one of Nehru's best parliamentary performances. It is doubtful whether any other Indian leader could single-handed have sponsored and carried through India's membership of the Commonwealth.

The importance which he attached to the Commonwealth as such is indicated by the fact that, under him, the Indian External Affairs Ministry—of which he retained charge during the whole of his premiership—had as its two top officials both a 'foreign secretary' and a 'commonwealth secretary' with their appropriate departments.

Nehru remained a faithful adherent of the Commonwealth idea to the day of his death, though of course his steadfastness was not entirely a matter of idealism or warm-hearted sentimentality. There were certain practical advantages to be gained for India, just as certain benefits accrued to the other members of the Commonwealth, and especially to the United Kingdom which still had a large investment in India and an important resident British community in the country. During the last days of British India, when the Indian Independence Act was in the drafting stage, the British business community in India had been much concerned as to whether they should ask for a formal commercial treaty between Britain and India. Wisely, they decided not to do so (a decision that was considerably influenced by the late Sir Stafford Cripps), and in the result they have had no cause to feel aggrieved or that they were being discriminated against. But the fact that Britain and India are members of the Commonwealth has undoubtedly induced a feeling of assurance in both countries that certain standards will be observed in such matters as trade, ability to enter and work in each other's country and the like.

Of course, economic ties between the two countries are largely independent of Commonwealth links. The sterling-cum-rupee devaluation of 1949 was not a matter to be decided on the basis of Commonwealth membership. Pakistan and Canada, both of whom were members of the Commonwealth, did not devalue. Essentially the decision affected the Sterling Area, which, in important respects, overlaps the Commonwealth. The resolve that the rupee should follow the pound derived from the close trade ties between India and Britain. Devaluation was debated in the Constituent Assembly in New Delhi on October 5 and 6, 1949, India's decision being defended by the then Finance minister, the late Dr John Matthai. He said:

The essence of the Sterling Area is that all the hard currency resources earned by the members of the Sterling Area are pooled and all the members have the right to draw upon the central reserves for meeting their deficits in respect of dollar resources. It so happens that next to the UK we are the country which makes the biggest demands upon these central reserves. . . . We are not a net contributor; we are a net beneficiary. So long as there is a maladjustment in our monetary relations with hard currency countries, there is not the slightest doubt that it is to our interest to remain in the sterling area. . . . It is a very difficult thing to build up trade connections. It is a fairly easy thing to destroy them.[1]

Enlightened self interest undoubtedly played a big part in Nehru's desire to keep India in the Commonwealth, though this in no way detracts from the credit that must be his for gaining acceptance of the proposal with apparently so little trouble. There were other practical considerations which must have been in his mind, apart from those which have been touched on above. There are many Indians in other parts of the Commonwealth—Africa, the Far East, the Caribbean, the South Sea Islands, and so on. They represent important minorities who by now have largely been absorbed into the local scene. Their ties with India are becoming more tenuous as time goes on, and with the progressive withdrawal of Britain from what were once colonies and dependencies under the direct rule of Whitehall, these groups frequently feel themselves friendless and insecure. Nehru always felt strongly about the alleged discrimination against his fellow countrymen in the former colonial empire, but he was powerless to do anything very positive about it. Behind-the-scenes personal talks in the friendly atmosphere of a Commonwealth Conference offered perhaps the best opportunity of drawing attention to grievances.*

Furthermore, Nehru was much too shrewd a statesman to fail to take into account the possible effect on India's position if Pakistan opted for Commonwealth membership and India did not. At the time he had to make his decision, the Kashmir dispute was still fairly new, and though he would never have conceded that the dispute concerned anybody other than India, Pakistan and the United Nations, he was anxious—because of Kashmir, if for no other reason—to keep open his lines of communication in all directions. The Commonwealth was one such, and his general attitude to it is probably best

* In a discussion in the Lok Sabha, December 5, 1955, on the Indian Citizenship Bill, Nehru strenuously denied that India was giving anything approaching reciprocal rights of citizenship to South Africa which was, at that time, a member of the Commonwealth. On the contrary, neither South African citizens nor South African goods could enter India. But 'in regard to the United Kingdom the privileges that Indian nationals have there are very great. In fact, they have almost all the privileges that the British people themselves have. In regard to other countries the privileges are more limited.'

expressed in the closing words of his address to the Commonwealth Parliamentary Conference when it met in New Delhi in
December 1957.

> What strikes me about the Commonwealth is not so much
> the points of likeness, which are many, of course—otherwise
> we would not be together—but rather the points of differ-
> ence which have not been allowed to come into the way of
> our meeting, conferring, consulting and co-operating with
> each other in a large measure. And if that is good for the
> Commonwealth, it should be good for others also, and good
> for the world at large.

The Suez Crisis

The two or three years following 1949, when India resolved to
remain in the Commonwealth, was the honeymoon period of
India's newly found independence. They were also the years
when Nehru was at the height of his personal and political
authority. But it was hardly to be expected that things would
go on so smoothly for ever. A major rift occurred in 1956 when
India, along with other parts of the Commonwealth, was
highly critical of the British government's action over Suez.
This episode falls into two phases: first, Nasser's decision to
nationalise the Canal; and secondly, the Anglo-French armed
action against Egypt. Both had implications for the Commonwealth of which India was an important member and for
which the Suez Canal was an essential communications-link.

There had been a Commonwealth Prime Ministers
Conference in London between June 27 and July 6, 1956. On
his way back to India, Nehru broke his journey to have talks
both with Tito and Nasser on the Adriatic island of Brioni.
While their discussions were in progress, Nasser received the
unwelcome news that American and British financial assistance
for the construction of the Aswan High Dam, upon which he
had been confidently relying, would not be forthcoming. The
two countries were to have made an initial contribution of
$70 million–$56 million from the USA and $14 million from the
UK. The latter was no good without the former. As the decision
to withdraw the offer was taken on the personal initiative of the
late John Foster Dulles, the scheme for western assistance was

scrapped and Soviet aid substituted. Whether the US secretary
of state was wise or not is by now so much water under the
bridge and of only limited relevance to this book. According
to Sir Anthony Eden, Britain was informed, not consulted.[2]
On July 26, Nasser seized the Canal, one of his declared objectives being that its revenues would help to finance the Aswan
project.

This brief outline of the opening rounds of the Suez dispute
is necessary because, then and later, Asian (and especially
Indian) reactions to the affair were of prime importance. It
also enables us to note Nehru's unequivocal denial to sugges-
tions that he had been made privy to Nasser's plan during the
Brioni meeting. On July 31, he told the Lok Sabha: 'the recent
decision of the Egyptian Government in regard to the Suez
Canal first came to my knowledge from the reports in the press
after my return to Delhi'. No more was heard of an insinuation
that was quite out of character for a man of Nehru's scruples.

But it very soon became clear that Indian opinion looked at
the response in London and Paris to Nasser's nationalisation
plans through a very different pair of spectacles from those which
were used in the West. The Indian press was almost unani-
mously hostile and, generally speaking, was more critical than
Nehru himself. Commenting on a broadcast in support of
British policy by Sir (then Mr) Robert Menzies, the Australian
prime minister, C. Rajagopalachari (a former governor-
general and a friend of Britain) said it was 'the true voice of
British colonialism speaking from the grave'.[3] Feeling was
running high over reports of French and British military preparations. There also began to be talk of India's leaving the
Commonwealth. At that time Egypt still enjoyed a considerable
reputation in India and Nasser had won Nehru's friendship and
respect by his apparently progressive policies. To those Indians
who take a simple black and white view of international affairs,
Nasser's seizure of the Canal seemed merely an act of deferred
and retributive justice. 'In the past', said a triumphant Nasser,
'we were kept waiting at their offices—the offices of the High
Commissioner and the British Ambassador. Today . . . they
take us into account.'[4] This brand of political rhetoric has a
strong appeal almost anywhere in the Middle East or Asia
today.

After Nasser's coup of July 26, Nehru stated India's position in regard to the Canal. India was not a 'disinterested party; she was a principal user of the waterway and her economic life and development was not unaffected by the dispute', he told the Lok Sabha on August 8. He warned against settlement of the dispute by force, and spoke about Asia's bitter colonial memories. There was no reference to the fact that in June 1956 Britain had faithfully kept the agreement with the Egyptian government and withdrawn its remaining forces from the Canal zone, and that in any case the Canal concession was due to expire in 1968; nor to the fact that the Egyptian dictator had abruptly and unilaterally repudiated an agreement of long international validity. The government of India, however, hesitantly accepted an invitation to an international conference in London 'having satisfied themselves that their participation will not injure the interests of the sovereign rights and dignity of Egypt'. The omission of Burma and Yugoslavia was regarded in Delhi as particularly regrettable, and it is fair to say that Nehru showed unusual solicitude for those countries which were least affected by the expropriation of the Canal and not very much for those which were. The whole issue had now been lifted to a highly charged emotional level in which considerations of equity received only scant regard.

India joined the London Conference, which opened on August 16 with representatives of twenty-two countries. Its delegation was headed by V. K. Krishna Menon, then minister without portfolio. This was not a happy augury for Britain or for the conference, having regard to the air of impending crisis that was spreading daily. Menon has great experience of international conferences, he has a quick and subtle mind and, if he chooses, can fill the role of 'honest broker' to perfection. On the other hand, if he wishes to be noncoöperative he can rapidly turn a quite straightforward issue into a profound and complicated philosophical problem. Krishna Menon, it has been said, 'is known to some as Mr Nehru's trouble shooter and to others as Mr Nehru's trouble maker'.[5]

The first London conference lasted a week. Though invited to do so, Egypt refused to send a representative. In his opening statement for India, Krishna Menon said: 'We have reservations with regard to the composition and character of this conference, and we deeply regret the absence of Egypt from our midst . . . no final solutions or even approaches to final solutions are possible without the participation of the country most concerned.' From Menon's melancholic and complaining tones it might appear that Egypt had been deliberately shut out of the conference room. It is necessary therefore to repeat that Nasser had declined the invitation to attend. On behalf of India, Menon submitted a somewhat involved plan which the conference found unacceptable and instead adopted a scheme for international control and operation. This was opposed by the USSR and by India, Ceylon and Indonesia. Nevertheless, the conference despatched a mission of five under the leadership of Menzies to explain the proposals to Nasser in Cairo, where they argued without success from September 3 to 9. But Nehru told the Lok Sabha he thought the reply of the Egyptian government had opened the way to further negotiations.

Meanwhile, John Foster Dulles had been giving the now rapidly deteriorating situation his somewhat erratic attention. He proposed the creation of a Canal Users Association— though how this was to be made more acceptable to Nasser than any other form of international control was never explained. In any case it did not matter. The proposal was shortlived, its author blandly repudiating it the day following Sir Anthony Eden's commendation of the project to the House of Commons. It was in these unpromising circumstances that the second conference reconvened in London on September 19. Pakistan, Japan and Ethiopia now joined India, Russia, Ceylon and Indonesia in opposition to a Users Association. However unpalatable to some sections of British opinion, and however distasteful Krishna Menon's posturing might be, Nehru's original assessment of the situation had been right. The tide of Afro-Asian opinion was now flowing strongly behind Nasser.

In the circumstances, it was not surprising that this second conference should have been one of the shortest international gatherings on record. It lasted only two days—just about long enough to wind up its affairs. India did not attend, though it can truthfully be claimed that its government was making considerable efforts to bring the disputants to the conference table on a different basis. Speaking in the Lok Sabha on Sep-

tember 13, Nehru described the Users Association as an
instrument of force rather than negotiation which could only
bring about 'an imposed decision'. On September 25, the
Indian government circulated proposals for 'a peaceful settlement'. Krishna Menon followed this up with visits to Cairo,
New York and London in his role of 'honest broker', but to no
avail. Under Sir Anthony Eden, the British government took
the view that the only basis for negotiation was for Egypt to
return to the solemn international agreement which it had
repudiated. Sir Anthony Eden began to compare the Egyptian
dictator's actions with those of Hitler and Mussolini twenty
years before—which, whatever the morality of the matter may
be, was not, politically speaking, comparing like with like.
So far as the prospect of a settlement by conference was
concerned, the end of the road had been reached.

The next move was to refer the matter to the Security
Council of the United Nations. Foster Dulles, whose actions
by now had become quite inexplicable, refused to sponsor, or
even support, an Anglo-French resolution; nonetheless the
British government asked the Council on September 23 to take
cognisance of the situation which had arisen as a result of the
action of the Egyptian government 'in bringing to an end the
system of international operation of the Suez Canal'. The
debate took place on October 5, and for several days preceding
and following the event there was intense diplomatic activity
in which Krishna Menon was prominent on behalf of India.
He put in writing proposals which he had previously canvassed
in London and Cairo, and they undoubtedly carried the
approval of Pandit Nehru. The essence of them was that an
international advisory body, which would have only vague
powers of supervision, should be attached to the Egyptian
nationalised canal authority. We do not know how the proposals had been received in Cairo, but we do know from Sir
Anthony Eden that London examined and rejected them. This
was undoubtedly a considerable personal disappointment to
Menon and seemed to confirm his poor opinion of British
diplomacy generally. Oddly enough, he was, for once, batting
on much the same wicket as John Foster Dulles. On October 13
the Anglo-French resolution was put to the vote of the Security
Council. It was in two parts: part one, which was largely non-

controversial, was passed; but part two, which contained all the contentious propositions (such as payment of Canal dues to the Users Association), was killed by the veto of the USSR, exercised by its delegate, Shepilov. So ended the second act of the tragedy, which was now moving rapidly towards its climax. India's policy of non-alignment had enabled it to play a not unhelpful, if somewhat devious, part off-stage.

Ever since the Israeli-Egyptian war of 1948 there had been sporadic border fighting between the two countries, and ships bound for ports in Israel had been denied the use of the Canal. The relations between these neighbours could best be described as hovering belligerence. On the morning of October 30, Israeli troops crossed into Egyptian territory. This was the signal for Anglo-French intervention. Egypt and Israel were given a twelve-hour ultimatum to withdraw to positions ten miles distant from either side of the Canal, failing which British and French forces would occupy Port Said, Ismalia and Suez. We are not here concerned with the allegations of bad faith and collusion, or with whether the attack on Egypt was cooked up in London or Paris. The full truth will probably take years to emerge. What we are concerned with is the effect of the affair on the Commonwealth in general, and India in particular. The Israeli government accepted the ultimatum and agreed to abide by its terms. Not surprisingly, Nasser ignored the demand—with the result that the Anglo-French forces found themselves involved in operations against the Egyptians only. This, to put it mildly, made the affair look not a little suspicious. And that was how it appeared to most of the Commonwealth countries, whose high commissioners in London had been informed of the ultimatum to the belligerents almost immediately after its despatch. So had the United States, which insisted on an immediate meeting of the Security Council at which for the first, and so far the only, time Britain used its veto. There is no need to recount the details of the sad and sorry story of the abortive military expedition, the cost in life and property, the damage to the Canal by vessels sunk in its entrance, the sabotage of the oil pipe lines and the widespread confusion engendered by what we now know was a colossal miscalculation. But the resultant political balance-sheet was even more depressing, particularly in the writing down of that

indeterminate but important item which we may call 'Commonwealth goodwill'.

It is possible to point to some blatant inconsistencies and
contradictions in the attitude of the Asian Commonwealth
towards the use of force. Roughly speaking, its scale of values
is that if one Asian or African nation uses military force
against another Asian or African nation it is regrettable—
sometimes most regrettable. But if a European nation attacks a
member of the Afro-Asian community, it is a monstrous crime
for which no words are harsh enough. An attack by two
European powers on one Middle Eastern country clearly falls
into the latter category. Nehru was informed at first light on
October 31 of the Anglo-French action. The next twenty-four
hours was a period of hectic diplomatic activity in New Delhi
with much coming and going at the Ministry of External
Affairs. India stood forth as the spokesman of Afro-Asia and
Nehru mixed sorrow with his anger, of which plenty was in
evidence (though there was a notable silence in Delhi over the
Russian crushing of the rising in Hungary—a point on which
Nehru was later to be strongly attacked by critics within India
as well as outside). On November 1, in a speech at Hyderabad,
he said:

> I cannot think of a grosser case of naked aggression than what
> England and France are attempting to do. . . . I deeply
> regret to say so, because we have been friendly with both
> countries and in particular our relationship with the UK has
> been close and friendly ever since we attained independence.
> I realise also that the UK has made many liberal gestures to
> other countries and has been a force for peace for the past
> few years. . . . In the middle of the twentieth century we are
> going back to the predatory methods of the eighteenth and
> nineteenth centuries. But there is a difference now. There are
> self-respecting independent nations in Asia and Africa which
> are not going to tolerate this kind of incursion by the
> colonial powers. Therefore, I need not say that in this matter
> our sympathies are entirely with Egypt.

This was a fair summary of the attitude India was to retain to
the end of the Suez affair. The cease-fire came on November 6
and a mixed United Nations military force took over from the

Anglo-French contingents the task of policing the Canal. Later the work of salvage and clearing up the mess generally had to be put in hand. Of the then eight sovereign Commonwealth countries (exclusive of Britain), six volunteered to contribute units to the UNEF which by the end of 1956 had a total of 5,500 men, of whom 1,100 were Canadians. With varying degrees of enthusiasm, India, Pakistan and Ceylon volunteered to send contingents. Pakistan's offer was rejected by Egypt out of hand. This action, which underlined Egypt's previous refusal to receive the Pakistani premier, Shaheed Suhrawady, in Cairo, was regarded as a gratuitous affront by Pakistan which it has not forgotten. Ceylon contributed an infantry company of 150 men. For a country professing a strong faith in collective security, and which had been amongst the most outspoken critics of the Anglo-French action, India's response to the UN secretary-general's invitation to contribute to the UNEF was curiously hesitant. Krishna Menon laid down a number of hair-splitting conditions; but in the end India sent a substantial contingent which, by the autumn of 1957, had risen to between 900 and 1,000 men.

It took some time to clean up the mess which this crisis in British and Commonwealth affairs had left behind. Serious ill-health compelled Sir Anthony Eden to quit politics. His successor, Harold Macmillian, was admirably equipped by personality and temperament to restore Britain's relations with the United States and the Commonwealth to their old footing. As might be expected, the Asian members of the Commonwealth viewed the Suez episode with considerable misgiving and mixed feelings, and in each case their governments had to meet demands that they should terminate the Commonwealth connection forthwith. Bitter and angry words were spoken in their legislatures, but in each case the national leaders were able to dissuade the rank and file from any rash course. Nonetheless, the events of the autumn of 1956 led politicians in India, Pakistan and Ceylon to re-examine the terms and conditions of their membership which, as Dr Eayrs puts it, 'is not the result of a protracted process of historical development into which the elements of conscious choice entered hardly at all (but) rather the result of deliberate weighing of its advantages and disadvantages . . . having decided to enter the Commonwealth, they are all for using the Commonwealth'.[6] Generally speaking the critics argued that, by remaining in a Commonwealth the senior member of which had wantonly attacked a largely defenceless nation in the Afro-Asian group, they had incurred (in the modern jargon) guilt by association. Nehru had little difficulty in dealing with these charges, and invariably he countered them by arguing in favour of the need for increasing international consultation for which purpose the Commonwealth was well suited. It was regrettable that there had not been any such consultation over Suez, but no institution was perfect, and it had been India's privilege and honour to help in linking countries, to build new bridges between them and keep intact those bridges which already exist. And so on, in the idiom which a hundred Nehru speeches have made familiar to students of international affairs. Quite soon the rumpus over Suez died down, both in the Indian parliament and outside. But it had alerted India to a new awareness of its position in the Commonwealth. For the time being, such uncomfortable and disturbing matters as India's position in Kashmir were forgotten, though it was not many years before Kashmir was to raise in Indian minds the question of whether India should remain in the Commonwealth.

What lessons may be drawn from this unhappy affair? The first would seem to be that India and the other Asian members of the Commonwealth regard it as an 'organisation' rather than as a 'family of nations'—a cosy sort of concept still held by many people at the time of Suez. In the second place, given the need to make a choice, the Asian members find it very difficult to support armed action against a non-Commonwealth Afro-Asian state. (It is the present writer's opinion that, had the Suez operation not been called off by Britain and France, India and Ceylon would have left the Commonwealth.) Thirdly, Suez revealed the widely differing evaluations of the United Nations obtaining inside the Commonwealth, and in particular the power which the Afro-Asian countries are prepared to attribute to the UN in any dispute between one of their number and a western nation. The stance which India and the Asian Commonwealth countries assumed over Suez was, of course, greatly helped by the fact that both the USA and the USSR chose to support the Afro-Asian bloc in the UN. Likewise in Britain itself there was a large body of opinion which roundly condemned the Suez action. This helps to explain why, when the affair was over, there were few recriminations, though it is highly questionable whether many people in India remembered Mahatma Gandhi's dictum of 1922 when he said: 'India's greatest glory will consist not in regarding Englishmen as her implacable enemies . . . but in turning them into friends and partners in a Commonwealth of Nations in place of an empire based upon exploitation of the weaker or underdeveloped nations and races of the earth and therefore finally upon force'.[7] Those words were spoken at a time when the modern Commonwealth had hardly been thought of.

9

THE LANGUAGE QUESTION: UNITY AND DIVERSITY

AT THE TIME OF INDEPENDENCE there were many quite highly intelligent people who expected the English language press to decline rapidly and the vernacular newspapers to gain in importance. Precisely the reverse has happened. How is this to be explained? India has at least a dozen major languages or dialects and at least a score of others, each of which is spoken by several hundred thousand people. Approximately 165 million people speak Hindi, Urdu, Hindustani or Punjabi; a further 90 million speak Telugu, Tamil or Marathi; and there are probably another 90 or 95 million whose tongue is Bengali, Gujerati, Kannada, Malayalam, Oriya or Assamese. All these languages are specified in the Eighth Schedule to the Constitution, and with figures of this magnitude no one group really forms a minority. After them come a host of other languages and dialects. Nearly 3 million people speak Santhali and nearly 5 million speak Marwari. The pattern is infinite and varied, and Pandit Nehru was well aware that the 'language question' could be the source of much danger to India.

We should at the outset make clear what we mean by the 'Language Question' and distinguish it from the demand for 'Linguistic States', which is a related but really quite different problem. The demand for linguistic states is a claim that the boundaries of the various States of the Union shall be drawn up on specific linguistic and ethnic bases. During the twenty years before Independence, Congress sponsored a demand that the provinces (as they were then called) should be reshaped according to such criteria, instead of by reference to administrative convenience which was the chief test by which the British-Indian government had determined their size and shape. We shall revert to this subject; here it may be said that Andhra is an example of a linguistic State. It was created in 1953 in response to a demand for a Telugu-speaking enclave carved out of the then Madras State: a decision which Nehru almost certainly afterwards regarded as unfortunate.

The Official Language Problem

In contrast, the language problem centres on the question of whether or not Hindi shall be the official language of the Union government, whether it shall be the language of official communication between the States of the Indian Union and whether for all practical purposes it shall supersede English as the *lingua franca* of the country. These are questions which are regarded very seriously in South India, where Hindi for the vast majority is an unknown tongue. The attempt to make Hindi the official national language was to lead, early in 1965, to widespread rioting in South India and to several acts of self-immolation by young men whom the phlegmatic western world regards as irresponsible fanatics, but who are deadly serious in their beliefs.

Nehru sensed that Hindi could not be imposed on those parts of the country which did not want it without risking a serious political conflagration, and he was therefore careful to handle the whole of this delicate question with care, in contrast to the rather ham-handed way in which it has been treated since his death. He was not himself a natural Hindi speaker, and it may be presumed that he felt some sympathy with those of his fellow countrymen who did not regard Hindi as their mother tongue.

Perhaps we should here digress a little and explain what Hindi is and how it comes to occupy such an important place in the language structure of India. Grierson*, who may be

* Sir G. Grierson combined, as did many members of the Indian Civil Service, scholarship with civil service duties. His *Linguistic Survey of India* (Introductory volume, 1927) has never been rivalled. Vincent Smith in his *Oxford History of India* (1958) puts the development of Urdu clearly and simply: 'The various necessities which forced Muslims and Hindus to meet each other involved the evolution of a common language.'

regarded as the leading authority on the languages of the country, describes Hindi as the generic name for the group of vernaculars spoken in northern India. Hindustani is a dialect of Hindi, and has been greatly influenced by Punjabi. It became the *lingua franca* of upper India as well as its literary language. It was also the language of the Army. The name Urdu originally referred to the military bazaar outside the palace of the Moghuls at Delhi who, with the members of the court circle, spoke Persian. But, says Grierson, from 'the efforts of the ever pliable Hindu to assimilate the language of his rulers' there arose a dialect written in the Persian script and making free use of Persian and Arabic words. As time passed Hindi became more Sanskritised and Urdu became more Persianised, while a third language was added in the shape of Hindustani, which was written in both Sanskrit and Persian characters and drew its words from both languages.

Hindi and Urdu have many features in common, but since independence the tendency has been for the gulf between the two to widen. In Hindustani, which is the amalgam, many objects have two names (one Sanskritic and one Persian in origin) which might be used by either Hindu or Moslem, according to taste. After independence Pakistan began to cast out the Sanskrit words and India began to reject the Persian ones—a process which was encouraged by the broadcasting systems in both countries. On balance, those most qualified to speak would think that Hindi has been the chief loser by this process of rejection.

A composite Hindu-Moslem culture had always characterised Allahabad, Nehru's birth place. Allahabad was also the capital of the former United Provinces (now Uttar Pradesh) until it was supplanted by Lucknow in the 1930s. The United Provinces of Oudh and Agra were the largest of the units of British India, and the Nawabs of Oudh were considerable personages in the capital, which accounts for the strong Moslem influence there.*
Jawaharlal Nehru's father, Pandit Motilal Nehru, was well

---

* The late Nawab Liaquat Ali Khan, Jinnah's right-hand man in the making of Pakistan and a Punjabi politically based in Uttar Pradesh, made it clear to the writer beyond a doubt that Moslems in Uttar Pradesh feared they would have Hindi thrust upon them. The language issue was one of the factors in the creation of Pakistan.

versed in Persian and Arabic and spoke Urdu when he did not speak English. If he did not actually look down on Hindi, he was certainly indifferent to it. Such was the atmosphere in which his son Jawaharlal passed some of his most formative years. The younger Nehru grew up to speak mostly English, but was also at home in Urdu. When political considerations made Hindi important he had some difficulty in speaking it, and was never a great orator in the language. In fact Nehru carried within himself many of the elements which have gone to make up the present linguistic controversy, and that was why he approached the subject with manifest caution. He regarded it as political dynamite.

The constitutional position in regard to the language forms to be used is fairly clear. Article 343 of the 1950 Constitution provides that the official language of the Union shall be Hindi in the Devanagri script, but that English shall continue to be the official language for a period of not more than fifteen years from the commencement of the Constitution. Thus, 1965 was to be a significant date in the unfolding of the language dispute. Under Article 344, the president is authorised to constitute a special commission at the end of five years, and then again at the end of ten years, to examine the growth and development of Hindi and to make recommendations for its progressive use as the official language of the Union with a view to replacing English completely at the end of the stipulated period. An official Language Commission was set up in 1959 and reported to parliament the same year. A parliamentary committee studied its report and recommended to the president that English should be the principal official language and Hindi the subsidiary official language until 1965. After 1965, Hindi was to become the principal official language of the Union, with English continuing as a second official language. No restriction was to be imposed for the time being on the use of English for any of the purposes of the Union and provision was to be made for its continued use, even after 1965, for such purposes as might be specified by parliament for as long as was thought necessary.

No doubt 1965 seemed a fair distance away in 1959, and in any case Nehru could rely on his great influence in the Congress

Party to obtain an acceptable compromise between the claims of the various factions. In commending the report of the Language Commission to the Lok Sabha, he accorded a rather vague and indefinite status to English, which he urged should continue as an 'associate additional language' for as long as people required it, and he gave an assurance that there would be no imposition of Hindi on non-Hindi-speaking Indians. Consideration would also have to be given to members of the services who could not be expected to learn Hindi in middle age. English was greatly important, he said, 'because it is a major window to the modern world for us. If we close it, it is at the peril of our future.' He was patently anxious, not to mute, but to keep the public debate at a controlled level. But it seemed to some people that he was shifting his ground when, in April 1963, he told parliament that the assurance he had given about the use of English could not be embodied in legislation, and that it would be 'absurd and unconstitutional' to provide for the submission of legislation for approval by particular sections of the country. The critics pointed out that it was not the present they were worried about but the future, when neither Nehru nor Lal Bahadur Shastri (his then Home minister) would be in the cabinet. Further fears came to the surface when Shastri declared he was considering making Hindi an alternative medium for public service examinations which are at present conducted in English.

It is, in fact, this fear for the future which was at the root of the violence and bloodshed which occurred in South India in the early weeks of 1965. The government of India is on the horns of a dilemma; if it writes into the constitution the assurances for which the South is asking, it would invite bitter opposition from the Hindi-speaking North, where an even more serious situation might arise. The South asks for specific legislative guarantees which the Union ministers could not give without embroiling themselves with other important parts of the country. Nehru, who was largely personally neutral in India's language controversy, understood the quandary in which his administration was placed. In his wisdom, he preferred to leave the subject alone for as long as he could. He well understood that politics is the art of the possible. What triggered off the 1965 strife were some maladroit utterances on Republic

Day, January 26, by the new prime minister, Lal Bahadur Shastri, when inaugurating an Official Language Conference in Delhi.[1] Strictly speaking, he said, Hindi should have replaced English completely on that day, and he declared that henceforth the change-over to Hindi would be faster, though if this ever came in the way of national unity the government would 'be prepared to slacken speed a little'. He hoped that those who opposed Hindi would give up their opposition and come to realise that 'there was need for a link language and that language could only be the one which was most widely spoken or understood'. It had been decided to continue the use of English along with Hindi to avoid difficulty for non-Hindi speaking people, but the Hindi-speaking States had a special responsibility, and they should encourage the use of Hindi and spread it as fast as possible. There was need for the creation of new Hindi words and literature, and this task must proceed at both the official and unofficial levels.

The marked pro-Hindi bias of this utterance from the man who was prime minister of all India, and not just that part of it which spoke Hindi, was unmistakable. Its implications were particularly marked in the South. Here the reaction was swift and violent. There was widespread rioting, arson and bloodshed; the best part of a hundred lives were lost and considerable damage was done to Union government property, particularly to railway premises (estimated to have suffered to the extent of £750,000). There were two or three cases of men soaking themselves in oil and meeting an agonising death by self-immolation. Human beings do not perform such acts unless they feel very strongly about something. What was it? Any proper understanding of the deep passions which this subject can, and does, arouse is possible only if we remember that language is, before everything else, an inheritance acquired with difficulty by those who pass it on, enriched and enlarged, to their successors of the next generation. Language is one of man's oldest and most precious possessions. The substantial differences in the main Indian languages reflect the various civilisations which India has absorbed, layer by layer, for thousands of years and which today make the country a vast storehouse of anthropological secrets. Language is not just a means of communication; it is the badge of nationality, a clue to caste and the medium in which men worship their particular god. It has its place in the most sacred rituals of a man's life and becomes part of his being.

For all that they may have been clumsy in some things, the British understood this and were careful not to outrage any of these susceptibilities. They decreed that English should be the medium of communication for administrative purposes, except perhaps at the lowest level. So English was used in the central government, and between provincial governments as such, and between these and the government at Delhi. English was also the language of the courts of law and the medium of all higher education. The Indian historian, K. M. Pannikar, puts the matter thus: 'By going in for English, India joined a world community.' It could not be better said. Under the British plan, no Indian language was elevated beyond any other and the country had a *lingua franca* which gave it a link with the western world (where English was supreme) at a moment in India's history when it required to enlarge its horizons. Over a hundred and fifty years, most Indians of the upper and middle classes grew up to be bilingual and the English language became one of the chief ingredients of the thin cement which binds the subcontinent together. But today its unity is threatened. In the north and centre of the country is the great Hindi-speaking bloc, which includes Madhya Pradesh, Uttar Pradesh, Rajasthan, Eastern Punjab, and parts of Maharashtra and Bombay; in the south are the States of Madras, Andhra, Kerala, Mysore and others which cling tenaciously to their ancient Tamil or Telugu or Malayalam language. The dividing line runs across the middle of India. A cleavage over the language question threatens to sever the torso of a whole country.

This was a situation which Pandit Nehru always feared and which, by persuasion and moderation and his personal authority over the extremists on both sides of the language frontier, he succeeded in avoiding. His successors, lacking his deft and sure touch in this matter, have not been so clever. They have in fact set off a chain reaction of which the last has almost certainly not yet been heard. As has been explained above, Hindi is the Indian language spoken by the greatest number of Indians, but its use is by no means general throughout the country.

Furthermore, Hindi has no international usage and, so far as science and technology are concerned, it has a limited and somewhat crude vocabulary. But, though its critics describe it as an unbeautiful language* (inferior in this respect to Bengali, which has a literature of its own and a rich vocabulary) it has the merit of being spoken and understood by more Indians than any other Indian language. And herein, it seems, lies the strength of the Hindi case. Advocates of its greater use ask: what is the good of elevating to official status a language (English) which the millions of poor people who inhabit our country will never be able to write, speak or understand? Is it not far better to extend the use of Hindi which is already spoken in one form or another by probably 200 million Indians?

There is great force in this argument, but it ignores some practical considerations of which not the least is that, because of the inept way the matter has recently been handled by Nehru's successors, a large part of India is now emotionally engaged. Its opponents are therefore unwilling to listen to arguments in favour of Hindi, however rational these may be. They see only the fact that Hindi has no external use in commerce or diplomacy, that it has no scientific terminology and that, since the happenings of January and February 1965, it has lost any unifying influence for the whole of India which it might have had.

After the trouble subsided in southern India, an attempt was made to paper over the cracks of which the rioting had been the overt evidence. A conference of Union ministers and chief ministers of States met in Delhi in January 1965 and Shastri was subsequently able to tell parliament that Hindi would remain the official language of the Union, but that English would continue to be an 'associate official language' for all business to be conducted between non-Hindi-speaking States or between them and the Union government. A day or two later it was reported that Hindi was to be made an obliga-

---

* Yet the limitations of Hindi would appear to give it a certain charm. Discussing this point with me, an Indian friend—himself a Tamil-speaking southerner—mentioned that so deficient in the terminology of modern technology is Hindi, that the Hindi word for telephone exchange is literally compounded of the words 'the hall of distant voices'. This, of course, is not typical, but it is also not unbeautiful.

tory subject in schools in all States, so that Hindi, English and
the regional language would become compulsory in the non-
Hindi areas; while English, a southern language and the
regional language would be prescribed for Hindi areas. Other
considerations apart, one may be permitted to question
whether this is a tolerable linguistic curriculum for young
Indians to have to face. The effect of all these events has been
to harden opinion and to confirm the protagonists on both
sides in their most militant postures. Even that wise veteran
statesman, C. R. Rajagopalachari, was moved to say: 'The
battle must therefore not be for time, but for scrapping the
Hindi policy and for the *status quo.*'

Two further propositions were associated with the conference of chief ministers and, as they lead directly to the subject
of linguistic states, some mention should be made of them.
They were that consideration should be given to a scheme
whereby each State would have an 'equitable share' in the
recruitment of officers for all-India services, and that in the
competitive examinations for such services candidates should
have the option of choosing, as the medium of examination,
English, Hindi or any of the main regional languages of India.
No decisions were taken on either of these propositions, but the
fact that they had a mention in Shastri's report to parliament
suggests that the Union government had to do some hard
bargaining to get any settlement at all. Their feasibility is to be
examined; no doubt with the Indian gift for evolving formulas
to fit most problems, something will eventually emerge that
will be put forward as satisfying everybody. But to change the
examination system and to introduce State quotas into the all-
India services is to weaken one of the factors which helps to
hold India together. Had he lived Nehru would almost certainly
have had to face the language issue in a more acute form than
previously; but he would not have allowed the 1965 situation
to develop as it did, for he cared more for the unity of India
than he did for the supremacy of Hindi.

The Linguistic-States Problem

In the last thirty years of British rule in India, there had been
an implied recognition by the authorities that provinces

created solely on the basis of administrative convenience, and which ignored the more obvious divisions caused by language or ethnic factors, were perhaps not the best possible way of preparing the groundwork for the federation which was already dimly discernible as the ultimate goal of constitutional policy. Both the Montagu-Chelmsford Report (1919) and the Simon Commission of 1930 (which spoke with special authority on this subject because it recommended complete responsible self-government in the provinces) drew attention to the possible redistribution of administrative boundaries on lines more in accordance with linguistic realities. Also, in 1928, a committee of the Congress Party, under the chairmanship of Pandit Nehru, declared its strong support for a regrouping of provinces according to language. It was to be expected therefore that the party, and Nehru personally, would come to office with a compelling mandate to do some fairly drastic redrawing of province (now State) boundaries. But first the integration of the domains of the former Princely India had to be accomplished. This, considering the magnitude of the task, was done remarkably expeditiously by the late Sardar Vallabhai Patel and his right-hand man V. P. Menon, who has since told the full story.[2] However, as so often happens, a close look at the realities of a problem reveals it in a new light. In 1948 a committee consisting of Nehru, Patel and Pattabhai Sitaramayya (a past president of the Congress Party and its historian) examined the subject afresh in the light of the new conditions of free India. They reported in a very different sense from anything that nationalist politicians had advocated previously. 'When Congress had given the seal of its approval', they said, 'to the general principle of linguistic provinces, it was not faced with the practical application of the principle and hence it had not considered all the implications and consequences that arose from this practical application.' It was not the first time in the history of politics that theories which have seemed so attractive in opposition have been found to bristle with difficulties when an opportunity has arisen of carrying them into effect.

But following the partition of the subcontinent, the integration of the Princely States (especially the important State of Hyderabad) and the general upheaval following the creation of the two new and independent sovereign states of India and

F

Pakistan, there was a prima facie case for a tidying-up operation, for trying to balance linguistic with other factors such as
national unity, economic growth, financial viability and, if
necessary, in appropriate cases redrawing the frontiers of the
State to fit the conditions of the new India. In December 1953,
the government appointed a commission to examine 'objectively
and dispassionately' the question of the reorganisation of the
States of the Indian Union 'so that the welfare of the people of
each constituent unit, as well as the nation as a whole, is
promoted'. In the meantime, a considerable agitation had
developed for the creation of a separate State of Andhra for the
Telugu-speaking part of the Madras State. This had been very
successfully exploited by the Communists and had been rein-
forced by the 'fast unto death' of Shri Potti Sriramulu, which
gave a dramatic quality and nation-wide publicity to the
demand for an Andhra which would be separate from Madras.*
How much Nehru was influenced by Sriramulu's death, or
how much by skilful Communist tactics, or whether he lost his
normally steady nerve, we do not know. But in 1953, before the
Reorganisation Commission had begun to sit, he agreed to the
formation of the new State. The door was now open to any
other linguistic group to make a similar claim.

The proceedings of the States Reorganisation Commission,
which reported in 1955, probably attracted more public attention than any comparable inquiry of its kind. It received
152,252 communications of one kind or another from the
general public, including about 2,000 'well considered memoranda'. The Commission examined 9,000 witnesses, travelled
38,000 miles and visited 104 places. These were the statistical
dimensions of the undertaking, and they may be taken as a
measure of the interest which Indians take in the prospect of
redrawing the political map of their country. Such is the leading
Asian democracy when in action over something it is really
concerned about. The inquiry also revealed dangerous under-
lying fissiparous tendencies. In one of the closing passages of
their report the commissioners said:

* The fast is a form of political persuasion, not to say blackmail, peculiar
to India. Mahatma Gandhi used it to considerable effect to focus world
attention on specific matters.

It has been most distressing to us to witness, during the course of our inquiry, a kind of border warfare in certain areas in which old comrades-in-arms in the battle for freedom have pitted against one another in acrimonious controversy, showing little appreciation of the fact that the States are but the limbs of the same body politic and that territorial readjustments between them should not assume the form of disputes between powers. Deliberate attempts to whip up popular frenzy by an appeal to parochial and communal sentiment; threats of large scale migration; assertions such as that if a certain language group is not allowed to have an administrative unit of its own, its moral, material and even physical extinction would follow as an inevitable consequence; and finally incidents such as those in Goalpara, Parlakimedi, Ludhiana and Amritsar; all point to an acute lack of perspective and balance.[3]

In these terms the commissioners gave a vivid picture of the deep passions which matters affecting the autonomy of the States stir up. They recognised the dangers of the situation when they observed: 'One view which is strongly held by certain sections of public opinion is that only a unitary form of government and division of the country into purely administrative units can provide the corrective to the separatist tendencies. We feel however that in existing circumstances this approach would be somewhat unrealistic. Other methods have therefore to be found to keep centrifugal forces under check.'

The reorganisation scheme which the States Reorganisation Commission produced came into force on November 1, 1956, from which date the Indian Union consisted of fourteen States (embracing over 98 per cent of the population) and six centrally administered Territories (covering the remainder). There were no territorial changes in the case of Assam, Orissa, Uttar Pradesh and Kashmir, the borders of which are not likely to be changed in present circumstances. The one completely new name was Kerala, representing chiefly the old State of Travancore-Cochin. Andhra State was enlarged and renamed Andhra Pradesh, and to it was transferred the Telengana area of Hyderabad State. It contains a population of something over 33 million people who speak Telugu which, next to Hindi, is the mother tongue of the largest group in the Union. Bombay State was enlarged by merging the States of Kutch and Saurashtra and the Marathi-speaking areas of Hyderabad, and giving certain Kannada-speaking areas to the State of Mysore. The new State of Bombay thus brought together about 26 million Marathi-speaking and about 16 million Gujerati-speaking people out of a total population of about 48 million. In respect of its finances and of its area it became the most powerful of all the Indian States. The linguistic cleavage between the two main groups was later to lead, after much agitation and disturbance, to a division of the enlarged Bombay State. In May 1960 a separate Gujerati-speaking State of Gujerat came into existence with its capital at Ahmedabad; the rest of the State (overwhelmingly Marathi-speaking) became the State of Maharashtra with the ancient and honourable city of Bombay as its capital.

Kerala was formed to bring a majority of Malayalam-speaking people together. Its 15 million inhabitants are amongst the most intelligent in India, and of all the States it has the highest literacy rate. Its north-western part is a rich plantation area producing tea, coffee, rubber and other products. Unfortunately, it also has a high incidence of unemployment among its educated but fecund middle-class. The main points of political polarisation are the Congress and Communist Parties and the Roman Catholic Church. In 1959 it had a Communist government headed by E.M.S. Namboodiripad, a former secretary of the Communist Party of India. After a few months, and amidst growing disorder, presidential rule from Delhi was proclaimed. Kerala caused Nehru not a few headaches and many anxious moments. Ever since its formation it has been the problem state of India; but it says much for Nehru's patient faith in democracy that he continued, against all the evidence, to believe that it would eventually produce a stable government for this most troublesome area.

Needless to say, the States Reorganisation plan did not satisfy all the claims of groups and minorities. The Sikhs were bitterly disappointed that their demand for a separate Sikh State (now a Punjab Subha in place of the earlier projected Sikhistan) was not conceded, and that the Commission recommended the merger of Patiala and the Punjab States Union (PEPSU) with West Punjab. The government accepted this recommendation and took the calculated risk of having a more or less permanently disaffected state on India's strategic borders with Pakistan. Once again the technique of the political fast was brought to bear. Tara Singh, leader of the chief Sikh organisation, the Akhali Dal, began a fast unto death in August 1961, but abandoned it under conditions that were extremely damaging to his prestige and standing in the community. In Assam there were anti-Bengali riots in 1960, caused by Assamese claims that jobs in the State should be reserved for 'sons of the soil'; the introduction of Assamese as the official language also caused trouble, especially in the Cachar area where many inhabitants speak a language with strong Bengali overtones. In 1961, as part of an attempt to come to terms with the Nagas, a tribal people who have caused much trouble for India in the north-east frontier area, their territory was taken out of the jurisdiction of the government of Assam and reconstituted as Nagaland, the sixteenth State of the Union.

The muster-role of the States of the Union is now as follows: Andhra Pradesh, Assam, Bihar, Gujerat, Kashmir (on the Indian side of the 1949 cease-fire line), Kerala, Madhya Pradesh, Madras, Maharashtra, Mysore, Nagaland, Orissa, Punjab, Rajasthan, Uttar Pradesh and West Bengal. This compares with the nine provinces of the undivided British India which had been handed over to India and Pakistan in 1947. Of the sixteen States, five are either exclusively or mainly Hindi-speaking. If India has to accept division on a linguistic basis, it would seem that, in spite of everything, rough justice has been done.

But by 1961 obvious cracks had begun to appear in the thin surface of Indian unity. People had begun to talk of Nehru as 'India's last Viceroy' and to ask more urgently who and what came after him? Who would hold the country together in the future? Nehru himself was manifestly disturbed and at the end of October appointed a National Integration Council with himself at its head, specifically to recommend 'how best to weld India's many religious, linguistic and minority groups into a homogeneous community'. The council consisted of 37 mem-

bers including chief ministers of all the Indian States, leaders of
the major political parties, lawyers (for whom as a class India
has an exaggerated respect) educationists and scientists. There
is no evidence that the Council has achieved anything of
practical value. Within a few months of its formation C. N.
Annadurai, leader of the Dravida Munnetra Kazagham, a
party which advocates the separation of the south of India from
the north, was putting forward a demand in parliament for the
creation of an independent State of Southern India inhabited by
people of Dravidian stock. He wished to see India 'a comity of
nations' instead of a 'medley of disgruntled units'.

Where did Nehru himself stand amidst these swirling linguistic currents and local patriotisms as they came to the surface of
politically free India? Those who knew him would, I think,
agree that, while other people might feel themselves to be a
Punjabi or a Madrasi or a Bengali first and an Indian second,
Nehru was first, last and all the time and above everything
else, simply an Indian. As a country and an entity in the world
India was the be-all and end-all of his life. But he was always
prepared to try to understand the point of view of the man whose
district or tehsil were the boundaries within which his existence
was ordered. He expressed at length in *The Discovery of India*
(perhaps the most personal of his books) his feelings on the
subject. 'Ancient India, like Ancient China, was a world in
itself, a culture and a civilisation which gave shape to all
things. Foreign influences poured in and often influenced that
culture and were absorbed. Disruptive tendencies gave rise
immediately to an attempt to find a synthesis. Some kind of a
dream has occupied the mind of India since the dawn of
civilisation.'

Is it a dream of unity? The rule for India, as for other
countries, is that politics is the art of the possible; with this in
mind it is certain that Nehru was always prepared to make some
concessions to linguistic factors, regarding this as inevitable in
India's condition. But he was extremely sensitive to anything
that would weaken the authority of the Union government.
He was prepared to adjust a State's boundaries at the expense
of another State, and even to create new States. But he was not
willing to do this at the expense of the Union government.
Rightly or wrongly, he assumed that there would always be a

strong central authority able to maintain India's 'unity in diversity'. Thus he made the best compromise he could, but it remains to be seen whether it is one which will work. A federation is the most difficult form of government to manage.

And perhaps here is the point at which to make a mention of the other great division in Indian life: caste. Himself a Brahmin, Nehru's attitude to caste was critical on two counts. As an agnostic he could hardly believe in the certainty of being twice born; as a social reformer he must often have reacted sharply against many of the inhibitions, rigidities and limitations which caste imposes on Hindu society. Whereas Gandhi's attitude to caste was based mainly on compassion for the weak and the outcast (his weekly paper was called *Harijan*—'Untouchable'), Nehru's consisted very largely of opposition to the ritualistic side of the caste system. Yet, despite its condemnation by the Christian church and the critics in Europe and America, caste is by no means wholly bad, and over the centuries has been found to be a powerful factor in preserving the coherence and discipline of Hindu society. It is frequently supposed in the West that, because a man cannot automatically proceed by merit from one caste to a higher caste, the Brahmin is supreme over all others. This is to take much too simple a view of the functions of caste. It is true that castes have multiplied until there are now said to be over two thousand castes, all of which have sprung from the four main caste divisions of Hinduism which are: the Brahmin, or priest and learned man; Kshatriyas, or warriors; Vaisayas, or merchants; and Sudras, or servants and menials. These were the four main original hierarchic divisions adopted by Hinduism in the Vedic period of Indian history. One authority has aptly described caste as making for morals and good order and being 'in fact the vehicle in which almost everything of permanent value in Hinduism was carried forward'.[4]

Much of the harshness and the quite revolting sacrificial rites, which the early writers on caste describe, have long since been removed from the system. Its main surviving blemish has been 'untouchability' and this Nehru quite early on determined to eradicate—as far as such a concept can be banished by legislative enactment. A number of the articles of the Indian

Constitution were accordingly devised to protect the position of
the scheduled castes and tribes and other backward classes.
The framing of these was the responsibility of the drafting
committee of the Constituent Assembly. By an odd twist of
fate, the chairman of this committee was the late Dr B. R.
Ambedkar, India's most distinguished Untouchable, a leader
of the scheduled castes and a lawyer of considerable reputation.
In pre-independence days Ambedkar had been a strong
critic of the Congress Party and a lesser man than Nehru might
have hesitated before appointing him to this highly responsible
post in the new India.

It is difficult to define untouchability briefly or positively.
Perhaps the easiest way is to mention some of the things which
the Indian Constitution prescribes as being necessary to protect
the scheduled castes against oppression by caste Hindus.
They include a provision that religious institutions are to be
open to all classes and sections of Hindus, and that there be
no disability or conditions with regard to access to shops,
restaurants, hotels, or to places of public entertainment or
resort to bathing ghats or to the use of wells. There can be no
denial of admission to educational institutions maintained by
the state, which must also consider the claims of the scheduled
castes in making appointments to the public services. The
scheduled castes are to enjoy special representation in parliament and the States legislatures for a period of at least twenty
years from the date of inaugurating the Constitution.

From this catalogue, it might be inferred that most of the
wrongs of which the low caste Hindu could reasonably com-
plain are essentially restrictive, or prohibitory, in character.
The Indian Constitution may enshrine noble sentiments in the
lofty languages of freedom and equality, but that this was in
itself insufficient to change practices which had been going on
from time immemorial was made clear by the passing of the
Untouchability (Offences) Act which Nehru's government
brought into force in the middle of 1955. This piece of legislation particularises what is an infringement of the heavily
generalised principles of the Constitution, and translates them
into cognisable offences under the common law. Thus, for
example, the act lays down penalties for refusing to sell goods
or render services to a Harijan because he is a Harijan; for

molesting, injuring or annoying a person, or organising a boycott or taking part in the excommunication of a person who has exercised the rights accruing to him as a result of the abolition of untouchability. There are many other provisions, especially relating to temple entry.

According to the 1961 census there are 65 million scheduled caste members and 30 million members of scheduled tribes in India. Apart from the humanitarian aspect of their situation, they are obviously an important electoral element which no party claiming to be fully representative of the people can afford to ignore. Caste, as well as having a religious basis, also embraces some of the features of the medieval craft guilds and there is evidence that caste is becoming increasingly important in politics, especially at election time and amongst the rural voters. In dealing with the problem of untouchability, Nehru was doubtless fully alive to the political importance of the usually meek and submissive low caste members of the community.

Apart from the guarantee of special representation in the legislatures for twenty years, posts have been reserved for the scheduled castes in the administrative and other services. Twelve and a half per cent of the vacancies filled by open competition on an All-India basis, and sixteen and a half per cent of the vacancies filled by other means, are reserved for the scheduled castes. For the scheduled tribes the reservation is five per cent in both cases. There are other concessions which relax age-limits, minimum standards of efficiency and other criteria for recruitment and promotion. Thus, in the public services certain small pools of employment are set apart for members of the scheduled castes and tribes, of whom about 331,000 were in government of India employ in 1962—many of them, we must suppose, in lowly or menial positions. The number is about equivalent to the total number of scheduled castes and tribes in one of the smaller Indian states, say Assam. But the mere reservation of a number of jobs for them does not automatically raise their status in the community. Rather the reverse—it tends to underline their backwardness. Nehru was fully aware that his legislation had made little impact on a problem which has consistently refused to yield to the zeal of the reformers.

The British made fitful attemps to abolish some of the worst
features of the caste system during the long period of their
rule; but by and large they were content to leave well alone,
on the grounds that they were averse to interfering with anything that had a religious foundation. So far as the subject
engaged Nehru's special attention, it is quite unreasonable to
suppose that he could substantially change, in a period of less
than twenty years, a code that has evolved over a span of at
least two thousand years. But he provided the legislative framework within which caste can be made less oppressive and therefore more acceptable. For the rest we may expect that India's
now closer involvement with the outside world, and the growing
awareness of their political power by the Harijans themselves,
will help to produce the conditions that are necessary for an
improvement in the status of the scheduled castes. In the
Discovery of India, Nehru briefly put on record his own understanding of caste, which he viewed as one of the three pillars
of the old Indian social structure, the other two being the
autonomous village community and the Hindu joint family
system. He pointed out that the idea of ceremonial purity had
always been extraordinarily strong amongst the Hindus; but
it had not always been consistent and had resulted in 'a growth
of exclusiveness, touch-me-notism, and of not eating and
drinking with people of other castes. This grew to fantastic
lengths, unknown in any other part of the world'.[5]

10

PARTY LEADER AND
HEAD OF ADMINISTRATION

PANDIT NEHRU had his first really serious illness in the spring
of 1962. He was then seventy-three years of age. His capacity for
getting around was slightly impaired, but otherwise the outward and visible effect of the embolism from which he suffered
was not very noticeable. Nonetheless, it was an unmistakable
warning to which he might have paid more heed had he not
enjoyed such abounding good health for most of his life.

The Succession Problem

But his illness did one thing: it focused urgent attention on the
problem of the succession. With the realisation that Nehru was
now a doubtful health risk, the Indian people suddenly
understood that the question of who should succeed him was
no longer just a matter for polite after-dinner debate but
might become of immediate practical importance at any
moment.

Nehru did not encourage speculation about the identity of
his successor, and in this matter as in some others he was withdrawn and uncommunicative. The Indian constitution makes
no provision for the office of deputy prime minister, though
until his death in 1950 Sardar Vallabhai Patel occupied such
a position and was so styled. After Patel's demise Pandit Pant,
Home minister of the central government and a powerful
figure in the political life of Uttar Pradesh, occasionally acted
as a sort of unofficial deputy prime minister and presided over
cabinet meetings during Nehru's absences from the country.

But he was in no sense a substitute for Nehru himself, and the practice was to defer decisions on all matters of importance until the prime minister returned to his desk and could give them his personal attention. Towards the end the effect of this was to 'stall' the administration far too often and for much too long a time. Since the death of Patel there had been virtually no one to complement Nehru, who overshadowed almost all the other members of his cabinet. This had both good and bad effects: good, because it meant that the prime minister's authority over his administration was real and complete; bad if, as it sometimes did, it meant that lesser ministers and some senior civil servants were unwilling to oppose decisions which they knew to be mistaken. The combined effect of Nehru's personality on his colleagues and a large, immovable and mainly uncritical Congress Party majority in parliament meant that there was very little of collective cabinet responsibility during the Nehru period.

Though the first of Nehru's illnesses did not occur till 1962, the period of what may be called his 'run-down' had begun somewhat earlier—say about 1960, though some people might argue that signs of decline were beginning to reveal themselves even earlier than that. But 1960 is a convenient date at which to fix this most important turning-point into the last phase of his life. By that time he had held the highest office in his country for thirteen years, and before that had spent practically the whole of his adult working life in the freedom movement. He was therefore a tired and much overworked man. He had never at any time made friends easily, and in these closing years, when most of his first Congress comrades had been removed by death, he became increasingly isolated from his fellows, though he somehow never lost touch with the masses. Like most other great administrative centres, Delhi has its own variety of private jokes concerning 'the establishment'. About this period the cognoscenti were in the habit of referring knowingly to the Indian government as the NIL Government— Nehru-Indira-Lal (Shastri). To those who looked more closely, this rather feeble acrostic was not without an inner meaning. In the first place it suggested that there was no effective government of India (which was what the critics alleged) and it also carried the implication that those closest to Nehru were

his daughter, Mrs Indira Gandhi, and Lal Bahadur Shastri—
which was, in fact, plain for all to see.

As the years went on Nehru, a widower since 1936, had come
to rely on his daughter Indira for the support and companion-
ship which a man in his position requires, and she ran with
devoted care that side of his life as a prime minister which
called for the intervention of a woman. Apart from being his
daughter and confidante, she was hostess and head of his
household, and her role in his affairs was doubtless very
considerable in these later years when his health was failing
and she herself had acquired a notable degree of political
experience. She was credited with political ambitions of a high
order by the gossips of Delhi who, in the next breath, added
that Nehru himself secretly desired to pass on the premiership
to his daughter who might prove an acceptable compromise
candidate in the event of disagreement amongst the main
Congress Party contenders. So far as the present writer has been
able to ascertain, there is not a scrap of evidence to support
these theories, though the fact that Mrs Indira Gandhi joined
Shastri's cabinet, as minister for Information and Broadcasting,
soon after her father's death may reasonably be interpreted as a
sign that she was being groomed for a more important post in
due course. It may also be taken as an indication of the Nehru
family's unquenchable thirst for political life, as may Mrs
Pandit's election for the Phulpur parliamentary constituency
in the vacancy caused by her brother's death.

But this is a digression. The question of Nehru's successor
involves some examination of his relations with the Congress
Party at this time and we must now proceed to look at these in a
little detail. There had been a general election in January of
1962, the broad result of which had been to confirm the
Congress Party in power, with 353 seats in the Lok Sabha
against 375 seats in the previous parliament. None of the
opposition parties reached even a fraction of the Congress
strength. The Indian Communist Party had 29 seats and the
Swatantra Party 22, against 9 previously held. The right-
wing Jan Sangh Party more than doubled its representation
from 6 to 14. But added together, these represented only very
minor gains; the overall result was a sweeping victory for the
Congress Party, and this in turn was largely a personal triumph

for Pandit Nehru who thereby rendered his last major electoral
service to the party.

The key contest of the 1962 campaign was in the North
Bombay constituency where Krishna Menon, with the backing
of the Congress Party organisation and the Communists, was
opposed by Acharya Kripalani, one of India's most talented
parliamentarians and a greatly respected figure in public life.
Menon suffered a number of disadvantages in a Bombay
constituency. He was a southerner unable to speak to his
constituents and agents in Hindi or any of the local languages.
He had been an expatriate from India for a number of years.
He had in fact many of the attributes of what is known as a
'carpet-bagger' in Western politics. The contest in North
Bombay was fought on the straight issues of Menon's personality,
his handling (as minister of Defence) of senior promotions in the
army and his influence on the conduct of India's foreign
affairs. Nehru defended his friend with almost fanatical zeal.
In the process he denigrated old colleagues, hurled accusations
at almost all parties except the Congress and made scathing
attacks on the local maharajahs, the Roman Catholic Church,
the press, the private sector, firms which had given funds to
the Swatantra Party, some of India's leading intellectuals—in
fact anyone who was courageous enough to say he did not want
Menon back in the cabinet. Finally, he made the matter an
issue of personal confidence, threatening to resign if Menon
were not elected. This, it was felt, was attaching rather too
much importance to Krishna Menon and his policies. Friends
noticed that a whirlwind election campaign, ranging over
thousands of miles and involving dozens of speeches, had taken
their toll of Panditji's physical strength. It came as no surprise
that soon afterwards he was taken ill and had to submit to strict
medical discipline. The nature of his illness was more serious
than was indicated in the press at the time, but he was able to
go abroad for short trips on several occasions later in the year.

A new council of ministers, or cabinet, was sworn in on
April 10, 1962, and its seventeen names included many who had
held office in the previous administration. It certainly gave no
clue to the succession which had by now become a more or less
open topic of conversation. The more prominent ministers—
Morarji Desai, L. B. Shastri, S. K. Patil and Krishna Menon—

were back in their former offices; and, broadly speaking, Nehru had preserved the balance between right and left which he was widely supposed to favour. T. T. Krishnamachari, after several years in the political 'outback', joined the cabinet two months later as minister without portfolio, thus bringing a considerable knowledge of economic and financial matters to an administration that was otherwise weak in this respect. But, though the Congress had been returned in much the same strength as before by the electorate, both to the Lok Sabha and the States legislatures, this did not mean that all was well in the party itself. It had been clear for some time that the party in various parts of the country was losing its momentum and sense of direction; that some of the high idealism which had once inspired its workers had evaporated; that the loaves and fishes of office (to use a term beloved of the Indian leader-writer) appealed more to the average Congress worker in the districts than the pure milk of Gandhi-ism (of which there is precious little evidence in the India of today); and that faction warfare amongst Congress groups in the States threatened the very existence of the party itself. It was alleged that the party was to a large extent living on past prestige and that its electoral successes were for the most part due to Nehru's personal hold over the masses, who continued to give him their unquestioning allegiance. No doubt in this mood of self-examination the picture was somewhat overdrawn; but there was also a great deal of truth in the spectacle it presented of a Congress Party breaking up under the weight of warring, disunited, self-seeking and corrupt elements.

One Congress leader who was considerably disturbed by these trends was Kamaraj Nadar, a non-Brahmin with limited English, who had been chief minister of Madras for some eight years and was rarely heard of outside his own State. He was particularly concerned because of the growth in influence of the Dravida Munnetra Kazagham, a party which strongly opposed the imposition of Hindi on southern India and advocated, if necessary, a complete separation of North and South India. At a meeting of the All-India Congress Party Working Committee, held in Delhi in the second week of August 1963, Kamaraj produced a plan the essence of which was that a substantial number of senior ministers in the Union cabinet and chief ministers in the States should resign their posts and go forth into the countryside and there proclaim the pure gospel of the Congress and devote themselves to full-time party work. The Kamaraj Plan was designed to revive the 'true spirit' of service amongst Congress Party workers, and to encourage a missionary ardour in place of the rather crude and vulgar scramble for the prizes of office which had become only too obvious in certain quarters. More significantly, Nehru perceived that this plan provided a useful backcloth against which a certain amount of political sleight of hand might be carried out.

Perhaps because there was no alternative scheme in sight, the Working Committee adopted the Kamaraj Plan, and Nehru was the first to tender his resignation. Needless to say it was not accepted—even as a token gesture. Contemplated in retrospect, the proceedings of this meeting of the Working Committee strikes a note of high comedy. Ministers are reported to have vied with one another in their efforts to resign; the scene must have resembled one of those card games in which the object is to get rid of the masters first. Nehru then unsuccessfully proposed that a subcommittee should be constituted to decide who should give up office. The upshot of it all was that it was finally left to him alone to accept or reject resignations according to his own judgement. In the ensuing few days the flow of resignations, which had started as a trickle, became a veritable torrent, reputedly including all members of the Union cabinet, all chief ministers and many other ministers in the States. India was in fact threatened with a complete withdrawal of its not over-abundant supplies of ministerial personnel. It had become the fashion to resign and, in all, three hundred ministerial resignations were received—three hundred hostages to fortune. This was a remarkable demonstration of Nehru's authority over the party.

On August 24, Pandit Nehru announced that he had decided to accept the resignations of six senior ministers of the Union cabinet and of six chief ministers of States. The Union cabinet ministers were: Morarji Desai (Finance), Lal Bahadur Shastri (Home), S. K. Patil (Food and Agriculture), Jagjivan Ram (Transport and Communications), Gopala Reddi (Information and Broadcasting) and K. L. Shrimali (Education). The first three were politically important. The fourth—Jagjivan Ram— owed his tenure of one rather prosaic cabinet post after another to his leadership of the Scheduled Castes in the Lok Sabha and the potential influence he could thereby exercise if there was a split in the Congress Party over, for example, the leadership and the succession to Nehru. On the whole, however, he was rather a minor political figure. The resignations which occasioned the most comment were those of Desai and Shastri: Desai because it was felt that he was opting to move from a somewhat friendless position in the cabinet to one of even greater isolation in the country, and Lal Bahadur Shastri because by now he had clearly become Nehru's most trusted collaborator and appeared to be giving this up to engage in a nebulous and undefined exercise in aid of the party. But Shastri's sojourn in the wilderness was destined to be of short duration. He was recalled to the cabinet a few months later as minister without portfolio to relieve the prime minister of some of his work. This suggested that Lal Bahadur Shastri was leading the field for the succession. By temperament, upbringing and environment Nehru and Morarji Desai were poles apart and it was no secret that their relationship had been considerably strained for some time past. In the days of the freedom campaign, Morarji Desai was much closer in thought to Mahatma Gandhi or Sardar Patel than to Nehru. One effect of the Kamaraj Plan had been to remove Desai from the centre to the periphery of Congress politics. Had Nehru cleverly foreseen this possible consequence? Or had Desai been a bigger political simpleton than seemed possible for a man of his long experience? These were the questions that people were now asking.

The evidence on the point is inconclusive, but the disadvantage at which Desai was now placed became evident soon enough. T. T. Krishnamachari was quickly appointed to his place as Finance minister. Desai's political reputation had been made as chief minister of Bombay which he had governed according to firm and somewhat puritanical principles, applied with considerable success. In return for the general efficiency of his administration, people were prepared to tolerate his fanatical devotion to such dubious propositions as prohibition. But following his promotion to Delhi, the State of Bombay, after much travail, had been divided into the two separate States of Gujerat and Maharashtra. The politics of western India had changed considerably in the course of two or three years. One of the points on which Desai was strongly criticised (by Nehru amongst others) was that he continued to interfere in controversial Bombay affairs—usually on the losing side—after he had quit the local scene. The centre piece of the Kamaraj Plan was that the resigning ministers should go out and work amongst the people; but this presupposed that the people were willing to be the recipients of such attentions. Unhappily, the citizens of Bombay, or rather that part of it which had become Gujerat, once again demonstrated that there is no such thing as gratitude in politics; they quickly showed that they wanted none of Desai's attentions and he thereby became the first and most important casualty of the Kamaraj Plan. There were others, S. K. Patil, for example, but he was soon back in office, and in any case he was not a serious contender for the premiership. Strong pressures were probably brought to bear to secure Desai's resignation but, assuming that he ultimately aspired to be prime minister of India, his agreeing to resign was a tactical blunder at a significant moment in the struggle for power in Delhi. Politics rarely affords a second chance, as was proved in January 1966 when Desai lost the contest to succeed Shastri. But it is unfortunate that India should be deprived of the services of a man who, whatever his faults or foibles, is a first-class administrator.

Desai's voluntary exile and his failure to secure a place (on such terms as he would accept) in the Shastri government which came to office after Nehru's death, prompt some reflections on the role of the State and the Union, or central, politician respectively. Success in one capacity is by no means a guarantee that it will automatically follow in the other. The minister who forsakes a cabinet post in a State for one at the centre takes certain risks. All too often he finds that he has to start again from the beginning and that it is quite a long time before he begins to make an impact on parliament. Despite a rather stiff-necked and aloof bearing, Desai had at last established himself with the more conservative elements in the Lok Sabha and had shown a growing mastery over the technical intricacies of his ministry. Nehru had never had to do this; he had served no parliamentary apprenticeship. He started at the top and remained there, which is why he sometimes appeared not to understand the problems of those who were lower down in the hierarchy. One of the charges that was frequently brought against Nehru was that he did not encourage younger men to come forward and qualify themselves for office. The allegation was not spelt out in detail, and it was never specified who had been kept back by his supposed indifference to the rising generation. Jai Prakash Narayan and Asoka Mehta (now deputy-chairman of the Planning Commission) were names of leading Indian socialists who were sometimes mentioned as being of ministerial material, but doubtless they had their own reasons for wishing to remain outside government. Nehru was not in any way averse to using non-party, non-political talent if it was available and when it was necessary; two of his best known Finance ministers, the late Dr John Matthai and Shri C. D. Deshmukh, had no previous association with the Congress Party, nor had Gopalaswami Aiyanger who was a provincial civil servant before entering the cabinet as minister for Railways and Communications.

One of the questions which Nehru's death has posed is whether the centre of government will continue to enforce the same authority and respect as before, to exercise the same fascination and exude the same glamour, or whether these qualities will now pass in larger measure to the States to attract young men of talent and political ambition. There may well be some shift towards the States in the balance of power as between them and Delhi, but this is likely to be of a very minor character. The Indian Constitution is so framed as to give the Union government strong centralising powers, which Delhi has not hesitated to use in Kashmir and Kerala, for example—though for different reasons.

Constitutional experts are divided on whether India is a unitary state with subsidiary federal features, or a federal state with subsidiary unitary features. The question is one of absorbing interest to constitutional lawyers and scholars, but the ordinary man is content to know that supreme power is not going to be whittled down in favour of the States. What is more, the Congress Party—which is the vehicle by which power can be reached—is geared to Delhi. Professor Morris-Jones, referring to the federalism of Indian politics, says:

> Congress itself is a highly federal body. Sometimes the High Command has been able to dictate to the party in a State—even shaping the formation of a Congress Government. But on other occasions Pradesh Congress Committees have been tails which wagged the dog in Delhi. Above all, perhaps, the history of Congress has practically demanded a continuous tension—except at points that were under the immediate control of Nehru—between government and party or between the party's ministerial and organisational 'wings'.[1]

For the present then, and for as long ahead as can be foreseen, the road to political power proceeds via Delhi. And it was there that the succession to Nehru was settled after his death, albeit with the endorsement of certain powerful Congress figures in the States. During the months of Nehru's decline, and particularly in the last few months before his death, the top-level decisions of the government of India had been made by a small group consisting of Gulzarilal Nanda, the Home minister who presided over cabinet meetings during the prime minister's absence; Lal Bahadur Shastri; T. T. Krishnamachari, the Finance minister; M. J. Desai, a senior and experienced civil servant who was head of the External Affairs Ministry; and Asoka Mehta, who was deputy-chairman and effective head of the Planning Commission. It is not suggested that these men acted as a government or as a committee of action; but individually and severally they took the decisions which had to be made during the long days of Nehru's deepening impairment. They kept the wheels of government turning. However, they were not the people who determined the succession. The suggestion that Nehru should have given a clearer indication of his preference regarding his successor seems incompatible, not only with his character, but with his views (so far as they are known) on how a parliamentary democracy should work.

A group composed of four prominent States Congress leaders which became known as 'The Syndicate', took charge of the business of finding a leader acceptable to all sections of the party in parliament and the country. The Syndicate consisted of Kamaraj Nadar (Madras); Atulya Ghosh (West Bengal);

Sanjiva Reddi, a former president of the All-India Congress Party and leader of the non-Brahmins in Andhra; and Lal Bahadur Shastri (Uttar Pradesh)—who was in the event to be elected to Nehru's place. The interesting thing about this caucus is the strength of the south Indian representation, reflecting the growing importance of the southern part of the country both in party and national affairs. It is generally agreed that Morarji Desai made little effort to make himself better known in the south or to commend himself to the party organisation at State and pradesh (i.e. district) level there. Even if he had gone out of his way to woo the southerners, it is unlikely that he would have secured the leadership in succession to Nehru; but without some support from that quarter he stood no chance whatever.

In reality, the party and the country were left practically with no alternative to Shastri, who seemed to have won Nehru's favour and who aroused the least opposition in the country and within the party. Most Indians could have placed their hands on their hearts and sworn, in the terms of a formula made famous in modern British politics, that he was 'the best prime minister we have'. If nobody could be said to be wildly enthusiastic about him, it was at any rate difficult to fault him on any of the tests by which Indian leaders are judged and his conduct of affairs during and after the Indo-Pakistani clash in the latter half of 1965 greatly strengthened his position. But in addition to the somewhat negative merit of just being acceptable to the party machine, Shastri possessed certain positive virtues. He was, indeed, a most efficient conciliator and mediator: an important asset in a country where quarrels, political and otherwise, are endemic. With his master, Pandit Nehru, he shared a reputation for personal incorruptibility, and this counts for a lot in a society in which corruption in high places is a commonplace of conversation, and in which the relationship of uncles and nephews is not always confined to the table of consanguinity. He was always a good party man, loyal to the leadership and doing rather more than the expected stint of routine and unrewarding jobs. He was reputed to be an excellent chairman of a committee; here he could exercise his gift for bringing together conflicting points of view.

Shastri's critics said that the danger was that he tended to

mistake conciliation for action. Having smoothed out a dispute
to the satisfaction of the party, or disposed of it by sweeping it
under the carpet, he was liable, his critics said, to regard it as
settled for good and all; whereas the chances were that he had
merely succeeded in evoking in the disputants a higher loyalty,
i.e. loyalty to Congress—in fact the same loyalty which had
been the chief factor in his own political life. It is hard to say
how far Indian policy during his relatively short tenure of
power was of his personal initiation, but the impression he gave
was of calm determination in a crisis.

This much at least is certain; the Shastri government conducted its business, however slowly, on the basis of genuine
cabinet consultation and not according to the personal pre-
dilections of a single man, however gifted or powerful. Although
Nehru was sincere in professing attachment to democratic
methods, he was at the same time very much a personal ruler.
In most matters he was willing to give conciliation a reasonable
trial, but he was by nature an impatient man and soon sought
to impose a decision. Yet, with sad irony, it turned out at the
end, when his powers were rapidly failing, that it was only with
great difficulty that he could be brought to the point of taking
decisions. The result was that important parts of the administrative machine became run down.

No two men could have been less alike than Nehru and
Shastri; and the latter must have been very aware of the difference between himself and his great predecessor. Nonetheless
he brought distinctive qualities of his own to the premiership,
not the least of which was his view of government as a process
of decision-making at the highest level in which all ministers
should collectively share.

The Indian Civil Service

Given the circumstances obtaining in India before independence, it was inevitable that for much of his life Nehru should
have been in conflict with the civil service. After he left Cambridge in 1910, he had seriously considered competing in the
Indian Civil Service Examination; but he decided against the
idea, which would at the time have appealed to his father who
was then a warm Anglophile. His decision not to sit for the

examination was to have far-reaching consequences for himself, for India and for Britain. He first attracted the attention of the authorities of his own area, the United Provinces, in 1920 when he was served with a notice of externment for allegedly establishing contact with an Afghan delegation then visiting India to negotiate for a treaty of peace. The externment order was subsequently withdrawn; but in December 1921 he was arrested under the Criminal Law Amendment Act at the time of the visit to India of the Prince of Wales, later Edward VIII. From that date onwards until 1945, Nehru was aware that the authorities, i.e. the civil service, were keeping a watchful eye on him even when he was not serving one of his numerous prison sentences, of which his wartime stay at Ahmednagar Fort was the last and the longest. He would have been less than human if all this had not coloured his attitude towards the bureaucracy which in India, as in other countries, is the backbone of government. In spite of the vast and sanguinary upheaval at the time of independence and partition, the British government was able to hand over the government of India to its successor as a going and working concern. This was largely because of the civil service it had created. At its topmost levels this was as good as any in the world and in its lower and middle echelons was quite the best in Asia.

It is difficult to say how much of this Nehru would have been prepared to acknowledge, though hardly necessary to add that his loyalty to his officials in matters of public business was impeccable. But it is less certain that he realised the extent to which the smooth transition from what he used to call a 'police state' and a 'law and order government' to a country which had as its long-term objective the creation of an Asian concept of a welfare state was due to a competent civil service trained in the British tradition of serving the government of the day. Moreover, after independence it was staffed right through by Indians, with the exception of one or two posts in the judiciary and in the technical services; there was accordingly no administrative hiatus when independence came in 1947.

A well-trained, competent and experienced civil service, able to take on the multifarious tasks of government, was a tremendous asset to India in the moment of its need. It has often been said that India was an administrative rather than a political problem and that as such the pivot on which all government turned was the district officer. Like most generalisations this is only partly true. The 'reforms' introduced by the acts of 1919 and 1935 (particularly the latter) had transferred increasing amounts of power into the hands of politicians elected on a popular if limited franchise. Prestige and influence tended to flow in the direction of the district headquarters and became even stronger as it approached the provincial capitals and the ancient city of Delhi itself. The popular idea of a young district officer ruling an area as big as Yorkshire was becoming less and less valid in the 'twenties and 'thirties—a period during which the politician acquired much self-confidence and a new importance in the scheme of things. Inevitably, in the political ferment of the time, the Congress Party and the bureaucracy found themselves in direct opposition on many matters. However high-minded professions of non-violence may be, it is very difficult for a campaign of 'civil disobedience' to be free from the intrusion of some physical violence which is only too likely to spark off bigger trouble.

Such a state of affairs did not seem to augur well for relations between the political leadership and the administrative machine of India when power passed completely into the hands of the politician. Yet, with the advent of independence, those Indian members of the various branches of the civil services on whom the administration now depended quickly proved they were just as loyal and patriotic as their political masters, and that their skills were essential to the running of the new India. Sardar Vallabhai Patel, an eminently practical person, was quick to perceive this. In contrast, Nehru seemed to retain to the end a feeling that the civil service had to be kept in check, and that a bureaucracy which had for long enjoyed a large measure of power and privilege would probably not willingly give it up. A senior Indian civil servant, H. V. R. Iengar, who served both the British-Indian regime and independent India, has related in a newspaper article how, at the time the constitution was being drafted, some leading members of the Constituent Assembly protested privately to Sardar Patel against certain privileges which it was proposed to extend to the former Ruling Princes and to members of the ICS and other members of the secretary of state's services. They claimed that Nehru was in sympathy with their case, though Iengar thought this was wrong and knew that the decision in favour of the princes and the civil servants had been collectively approved by cabinet. Sardar Patel replied to the deputation and Iengar writes: 'He spoke warmly of the great work being done by members of the ICS and other services after the transfer of power; some day history would recognise the part they had played in the preservation of internal stability after chaos had broken out in the Punjab and elsewhere. He added firmly that he would not be a party to breaking a pledge given to them either.' The writer adds: 'Likewise he (Sardar Patel) knew that not all members of the ICS and other services were equally deserving of praise; a few of them did not deserve any particular support; but in the overall context this was immaterial.'[2]

I I

A TRIAL BALANCE

WHEN NEHRU DIED in the early hours of May 27, 1964, grief was widespread, deep and sincere. And not only in India: its sorrow was shared by the Commonwealth and the whole world whose post-war pattern he had helped to shape. But time is a great healer and like all griefs, particularly those for the passing of men whose work would seem to be done, that for Nehru gradually gave place to a less emotional assessment of the statesman whom India had chosen for its favourite son.

For sometime previously there had been something in the nature of a conspiracy of silence. Although it was obvious that his health was precarious, it had been bad form to say so or to suggest that the administration was suffering because Nehru was no longer capable of carrying the tremendous burden that he had voluntarily placed upon his own shoulders over the years. Indians resemble the English in their reticence over matters of personal health, and in the ordinary way they do not regard age as a handicap either in politics or in business. But Nehru had clearly reached a point at which his judgement was faltering, and he obviously found it increasingly difficult to make decisions. A close observer in those last days said to the writer that if only Nehru were willing to delegate most of his work, and to ration his time and his energies strictly, he might continue to rule India for a long time. But, of course, he did not do either of these things, and would not have been the Jawaharlal Nehru that India and the world knew if he had done so. And so, though he did not die at his desk he died in office, full of years and honour and amidst the love and respect of his people. With his death, however, they felt able to speak more freely, and it was agreed that, like most other stories of human

endeavour, Nehru's services to India were compounded un-
evenly of success and failure. As a tailpiece to this somewhat
compressed narrative of the years since 1947, we might look
briefly at the credits and debits of the account.

When we are far enough away from his lifetime for the historian
to pass a proper verdict, it will probably be found that Nehru's
greatest gift to India was himself. This may sound trite, even
rather stupidly self-evident. But what it is meant to convey is
that, if Nehru had been a different kind of man, India would
have become a different kind of country. By and large, the
post-war freedom movements have been led (especially in
Africa) by men who value office for the power, prestige and
money which office confers, who consider themselves above the
law, whose decision-making is arbitrary and 'who have never
experienced democracy and know neither its philosophy nor
its history. . . . Men who claim to be democrats in fact behave
like emperors'.[1]

Nehru, however, valued his high office, not for what it
enabled him to do for himself, but for what it empowered him
to do for India. Thanks to the accident of history and the
organisational resources of the Congress Party, India is very
largely a one-party state; but it is not the kind of one-party
state in which all other parties are suppressed and political
opposition is killed off or driven underground. Nehru was alive
to the danger of the dominance of the Indian legislatures by a
single party and he took steps to extend the process of consultation—particularly in economic matters—with outside public
opinion as much as possible.* Nehru was no Mahatma and by
the same token neither was he of the stuff of which emperors
and dictators are made. He was liberal, humane, forgiving,
generous in his judgements and trustful—sometimes too trustful—and he brought these qualities to the task of governing
India, so making his country's administration, with all its
imperfections, one of the best in the developing world. In a
word, he personally set the tone for a government which (whatever its shortcomings) tried to rule according to the decencies
of life.

* Examples are the National Development Council and the Board of
Trade.

As a practical example one may take his attitude towards the newspaper press, both domestic and foreign. Subject to observance of the ordinary law designed to protect the individual from libel and defamation, the Indian press is as 'free' as any in the world. The representatives of the foreign press are treated with every consideration and are not subject to any restraints or discrimination because they are foreign. It is true that foreign newspaper representatives have not been particularly welcome in Kashmir or Nagaland, but the Indian newspapers have enjoyed no preference over them in this respect, and it is not unusual for governments to place some restrictions on newspaper activities in areas in which military operations are being conducted. In parenthesis it may be said that India's handling of the foreign press during the recent Indo-Pakistan clash was not very intelligent. But Nehru's line was that a responsible press was evidence of political maturity and that freedom was a prime condition of responsibility. The Indian press and the permanent representatives of the foreign press in India, he held, should therefore enjoy full freedom to report and comment on events in whatever way they liked. During his regime there were no press ordinances or official closures. Indeed, the only legislative action in respect to the press was the appointment of a commission to investigate matters of ownership and staff working conditions. In a more positive fashion, parties of foreign newspaper representatives have toured India as guests of the government examining and assessing the progress of the Five Year Economic Plans. In this and in other ways, the various ministries of the Union and States governments have shown a readiness to discuss their policies with inquiring journalists which is rare in Asia—and, indeed, in some other parts of the world.

Nehru's own personal relations with the press fluctuated a good deal. As a world statesman he was treated with respect, but not necessarily with adulation and least of all with servility. He was not an easy man to interview: when he was in a communicative mood he was prone to prolixity, while his silences, which gave the impression of taciturnity, could be embarrassing. He was not always pleased with the result of an interview when it appeared in print, or with the outcome of a press conference, but he accepted the rough with the smooth. The result was that he established a relationship between the press and his government which was singularly free from any suggestion of duress and in which the newspapers felt that their integrity was properly respected. It would be a fair statement to say that the Indian newspaper press is noticeably freer today than when Nehru came to office in 1947 when the remains of wartime censorship were still operating. The American political theorist, Walter Lippmann, told the last conference of the International Press Institute that a press monopoly is incompatible with a free press and that the latter exists only when newspaper readers have access to other newspapers which are competitors and rivals. It is much to India's credit that, in spite of its serious foreign exchange difficulties, it has never placed any restriction on the importation of foreign news and newspapers, by which readers of the country's own newspapers can check their sources of information.

'The unity of India' is a phrase one hears repeatedly in any discussion of Nehru's leadership of his country, and it has come to mean different things to different people. To many it meant, and means, the exercise of its authority by a strong central government over the whole of the country; some see it entirely in the context of territorial integrity; others again measure Indian unity in terms of language, culture, religion and the like. So far as the present writer knows, Nehru never spelt out exactly what he understood by the unity of India. He certainly would not have endorsed all the definitions that are implicit in the current dialogue on the subject, and it is doubtful whether he would have accepted in its entirety any one of them. Yet Indian unity—whether it became greater or less during his seventeen-year reign—is bound to be one of the tests by which posterity will judge him. Here we can attempt only a very provisional judgement, which must start with the simple fact that India possesses little natural unity and that many of the most powerful influences at work in the country are predominantly separatist in character.

For a long time Indian nationalist leaders, including Nehru, affected to pretend that these separatist trends were encouraged by the British for their own reasons; *divide et impera* was the allegation frequently made against the Raj. The survivors of the generation who made the charge know differently now. In the later years of the Raj, opposition to the British-Indian government provided a unifying focus for Indian nationalism. At the same time, by reason of the strong autocracy on which it rested, this government was able to give India a degree of unity which it had never before possessed, and could never have attained under any two-tier system of representative government serving both federation and its units, whose linguistic and other post-independence differences were likely to deepen their divisions. It would be idle to pretend that Nehru was unaware of all this; at the same time he was conscious that the nationalist movement had espoused, for its own purposes, any cause that looked like bringing grist to the political mill, including those lesser local patriotisms which on the long view were fissiparous rather than unifying. There were plenty of these in a vast country whose regions are, in some respects, as different as Russia and Spain.

Nehru's dilemma was that, as head of the government, he found it politically very difficult to deny the validity of centri-petal propositions which he had accepted during the long years of campaigning for India's freedom; yet, as prime minister, he was now bound to look at it through a different pair of spectacles. At best he could only temporise, as he did with Potti Sriramulu's fast unto death for a Telugu-speaking State in Andhra, which opened the way for other embarrassing claims of a similar kind. It is mostly by foreigners that he has been criticised on the subject of Indian unity, and it is mainly among non-Indians that one hears the suggestion that India has become less united during the seventeen years in which Nehru was at the head of its affairs. The fact is that it is very doubtful whether any Indian thinks of India's nationhood in dimensions that a European would apply to the same proposi-tion; for the Indian his country is a continent in which the part has always been at least as great as the whole—and in almost all cases more important in a practical sense.

Though it accorded with many of the essential ethnic and linguistic facts, the guiding principle of the British-Indian government up to 1947 in determining the size of the provinces and the shape of their boundaries, was administrative con-venience. As a popularly elected leader, Nehru was obliged to take other considerations into account. It was not long before local politics began to spill over into the wider field. The nine British-Indian Provinces of 1939 have become the sixteen States of today's Indian Union. *Prima facie* it can be argued that this is strong statistical evidence of the onset of the process of disintegration. But it can equally plausibly be contended that the creation of the new States has been at the expense of the old ones, which have thereby become weaker vis-à-vis the centre. For example, neither individually nor collectively do Maharashtra and Gujerat equal in influence and resources the former Bombay State, of which they were the two halves. The conclusion must be that the authority of the central government has been in no way impaired by the creation of new States; indeed, relatively speaking, it may have been strengthened. Where the centre has to move with caution is in its dealings with old and well-established States governments: Uttar Pradesh, Madras and West Bengal come to mind. These and one or two others represent the real framework of the unity of India, to which Nehru's contribution cannot yet be measured with anything like final judgement.

Similarly, only the most tentative opinion can yet be set down about Nehru's attitude towards the application of modern science to India's industry and defence problems. His interest in scientific matters went somewhat deeper than his occasional appearances at the annual session of the Indian Science Congress; and in addition to being prime minister and minister for External Affairs, he also held the portfolio for Atomic Development. This was no mere honorific; he took his duties seriously and like all professing socialists had great expectations of the manifold uses that might be made of technology. But India is a poor country, and among the factors of production the only real surplus it possesses is a well-nigh unlimited supply of labour. India's resources for scientific research and applied technology are correspondingly limited. Nonetheless, substantial progress has been made, and one or two of India's scientific leaders—for instance, the late Dr Bhabha and the late Dr Megnath Saha—have been quite outstanding in their particular subjects. As a matter of historical fact this is not a new development but has always been so; the individual

Brahminical intellect seems brilliantly adapted to the problems of modern mathematics and physics.

A layman is ill-qualified to say where India stands in the world pursuit of nuclear techniques—whether, for example, it is ahead of Egypt or how far it still has to go to draw level with China. Fortunately an expert opinion is on the record by which it is possible to make a rough comparison between the Asian contenders for nuclear supremacy. Kurt Mendelssohn, reader in Physics at Oxford, visited both India and China in 1963 and he described in a Third Programme talk how, at the end of this tour, Nehru was anxious to see him to ascertain what he thought about India's progress in science and technology compared with that of China. Between Mendelssohn's visit to the two countries, China had scored its resounding military victory in the Himalayas, and India was smarting under the sting of defeat. On the whole, Mendelssohn's findings show China to be ahead, not so much in actual achievement (though since his visit the Chinese have carried out two successful explosions of their bomb) as in its ability to organise limited scientific and technological resources to the best effect. To meet the Chinese emergency, Indian universities and government research laboratories had suffered a 20 per cent cut in their budget and, says Mendelssohn 'far from playing their part in helping their country, Indian scientists had been made to feel that, in the national emergency, money spent on science was ill-spent, and that they were not a help but a hindrance. Frustration and discontent were only too apparent'. He continues:

But even before the crisis, it had become clear to Western observers that some kind of malaise was hampering Indian science and technology. There were unmistakable tell-tale signs of this. One was the often depressing content of their scientific publications. It is not that the standard is low, but the subjects on which work is proceeding are hopelessly out of date. Again and again contributions sent to our scientific societies had to be rejected because they had nothing new to say. Another sign is the reluctance of Indian scholars, trained in the West, to return to India. This Indian brain drain went so far that a few years ago the Indian Government

started to exact caution money from scientists whom they
sent abroad.[1]

Kurt Mendelssohn considers that the trouble really starts in the
universities, whose spirit is that of Oxford at the turn of the
century. In the main, the Indian universities have become
cloistered academies with chairs of English, Sanskrit and Law
as the most important appointments. There is much regard for
status and not a little intrigue. But there are brilliant exceptions, among which the Tata Institute in Bombay is outstanding,
as is the Atomic Energy Research Laboratory at Trombay.
Mendelssohn concludes that it is not the know-how of science
that the Indian professors need so much as the know-how of
talking to their government. In the end, it is the job of the
politicians to make proper use of their scientists.

If we are to accept this assessment of the situation, it is clear
that Pandit Nehru did not achieve the scientific revolution of
which he often talked. Yet the record of the last decade is by
no means negligible. India's atomic energy programme has
hitherto been based on the assumption that its objectives would
be restricted to peaceful uses; but it is claimed that, with very
slight adaptation, its whole nuclear complex could quickly be
turned to the production of the bomb—a prospect which has
now become a matter of urgent discussion. There is in fact some
evidence that India's original plans were made with this
possibility in mind, and if this is so the credit goes to Nehru
and his senior nuclear advisers.

But before considering that aspect of the matter, we might
appropriately catalogue some of the progress that has been
made in the ten years since the Atomic Energy Commission
began its work. The Trombay establishment, which carries
out most of the Commission's investigations, is staffed by more
than 1,500 physicists and engineers and includes a 'swimming-
pool-type' reactor which became critical nine years ago.
There are also a zero energy reactor; a 40-megawatt research
reactor, built with Canadian collaboration; a prototype atomic-
power generating station of 20 megawatts under design; a
plutonium plant; plants to produce uranium-233 of thorium
of high nuclear purity; and a radio isotope production plant.
The atomic power programme includes a plant in western

India due to generate electricity in 1968, to be followed by
another one in the same region; a third is to be located in the
south and a fourth is to be set up somewhere in central India—
the whole to produce 3,000 megawatts of atomic power by
1976. India is also in a comfortable position in regard to raw
materials. The thorium deposits in the Chota Nagpur plateau
are estimated to amount to about 300,000 tons and a further
200,000 tons in the State of Kerala give India probably the
largest known thorium deposits in the world. History was made
some months ago when India became a supplier of boron
isotopes to the United States.

Whether India should, or should not, develop the bomb was
an issue about which Pandit Nehru doubtless thought a good
deal, but was not called upon to make a firm or final decision.
When he died in 1964 the Chinese had not yet projected themselves into the membership of the small and exclusive club
consisting of those nations which have detonated a nuclear
bomb. But a few months later (on October 24, 1964), they
exploded a device which gave them a title to be regarded as at
least an embryonic nuclear power, and the event changed the
whole balance of power and political prospect in Asia. For India
in particular, China's newly acquired nuclear expertise seemed
to bode no good. The new government of L. B. Shastri was thus
the inheritor of a fairly well advanced nuclear capacity, but
also of a policy in regard to its use that stopped short of taking
the crucial plunge into the world nuclear contest. Whereas,
during the Nehru era, the question had been largely academic,
it has since become a matter for practical political decision, and
any examination of Nehru's legacy to India must take account
of the fact that China 'has' the bomb and India has not.
Shastri said that India's policy would be to continue to direct
the nuclear programme to peaceful purposes, and there at the
moment the matter rests. But nobody in India supposes that it
will remain there for very long, and a demand for the extension
of nuclear activity into the military field is likely to grow as
China becomes more overtly a nuclear power. The chief
limiting factor is finance, though it is arguable that if China,
which is also a poor country, can find the resources to manufacture the bomb, so too can India. The moral, or Gandhian,
argument is less compelling and is not likely to become more

compelling as the years go by. But even supposing that a good deal of the initial cost has already been met in developing nuclear power for peaceful purposes, the financial outlay in making the bomb, and above all in providing the means of delivering it on distant targets, would be quite prohibitive for India whose economy is now mortgaged up to the hilt in support of its five year plans. Technically, the thing is perfectly feasible; financially it seems well nigh impossible.

But there are other considerations for and against. Against the manufacture of the bomb is the fact that, at best, India's role as a nuclear power could only be marginal. Assuming China to be the enemy, Indian cities are far more accessible and vulnerable to Tibet-based Chinese bombers than are Chinese cities to Indian bombers operating from airfields in the North East Frontier area. India, the 'anti' faction declare, must look to its Western friends for protection against nuclear attack. The people who think this way include most senior civil servants, defence service chiefs and those business men who have given serious thought to the matter. Above all, they contend, if India were to go for the bomb it would finally dispose of any hope of a reconciliation with Pakistan. Against this, the younger generation of soldiers and airmen, of civil servants and intellectuals maintain that India is not going to get a settlement with Pakistan anyhow; that Pakistan is now China's ally; and that China intends to use the bomb as an instrument of blackmail. This, they claim, presents India with a totally unacceptable situation. Far better, they say, to face the facts now and to get the bomb on the best terms open to India than to appear to acquiesce in a prolonged period of Chinese blackmail. They add that, if it comes to the crunch, India's friends in the West will accord only a low priority to its nuclear needs; and finally they argue that it is in Asia that India needs to uphold its position, which it cannot do effectively without the bomb. In other words, nuclear status, however limited, will give India a seat along with China at Asia's top table; in a slightly different context it is a variant of the British case all over again.

This matter has been dealt with at some length: first, because it is of importance in itself; and secondly, because it arises directly from Pandit Nehru's serious misreading of Chinese policy and intentions. This has left Indian thought in a state of confusion regarding certain first principles, one of which has assumed (quite wrongly) that no Asian nation, with the possible exception of Pakistan, would attack another Asian nation and that the only aggressors were the wicked and unregenerate powers (ex-colonial and otherwise) of the West. This, and the uncritical acceptance of the myth of a thousand years of Indo-Chinese friendship (broken only by the machinations of Britain during its long suzerainty over India), together with the illusions of the *Panch Shila*, thoroughly unfitted Indian public opinion for the hard decisions that would eventually require to be made. For this Pandit Nehru must share most of the responsibility—though it should also be said that he was the architect of a nuclear policy which could easily be redirected to the making of the bomb if it were decided to do so and the necessary finance were available. To sum up: in some respects Indian thinking, the course of which was largely set by Nehru, has naïvely assumed that the policies of certain other countries were devoid of all selfish or predatory motives. Too often, in fact, India has seemed and acted like an innocent abroad. One may suppose that the China experience, culminating in the manufacture of the bomb, has provided a sharp corrective.

There has been a good deal of discussion about Nehru as a socialist. He entered nationalist politics via the Kisan Sabha movement in 1916, in what was then the United Provinces. There is no evidence that he was a socialist at that time; indeed in the beginning he identified himself almost exclusively with the peasant movement under the leadership of Pandit Madan Malaviya, and only gradually did he get drawn into the wider web of Congress politics. He appears to have adopted the socialist faith gradually, and his formal conversion to it may be said to date from his protracted European tour of 1926–7 when he visited Britain, France, Holland, Germany and the Soviet Union. The tour was undertaken primarily in the interests of his wife's health, and while she made her headquarters in Switzerland he visited the other European countries. He represented the Indian National Congress at various gatherings, including the Brussels Conference of Oppressed Nationalities. In the course of his continental travels he met a great many leaders of minority movements who were invariably socialists. The two roles usually go together. His short visit to the Soviet Union impressed him greatly, and the newspaper articles written on his return show an unusual understanding of the position Russia was destined to occupy before very long in world affairs. Writing in the volume of essays which was published in honour of Nehru's seventieth birthday in 1959, the editor, Rafiq Zakaria, says of his return from this European trip 'he came back not so much a nationalist as a socialist determined to give a new content and meaning to Indian nationalism, as much economic as political'.[3] No attempt to assess his influence on affairs since 1947 would be complete without some consideration of what this meant for Indian commerce and industry.

For a committed socialist, Nehru's attitude to business was curiously ambivalent. It frankly disappointed his fellow socialists, and mystified—without encouraging—the private sector which, because it did not clearly understand his philosophy of pragmatism, remained suspicious of his policies. The business community asked for specific undertakings; in response Nehru declared that his approach to this or that problem was 'pragmatic' (an oft-used word of his). If the best way seemed to be to proceed by private enterprise, then private enterprise it would be; if, on the other hand, private enterprise seemed unsuitable, state ownership and management would be applied. On both sides there was a failure to communicate and organised Indian business was often exasperated by what it regarded as imprecise and meaningless arguments. British business, which formed the largest element in the foreign enclave, had had more experience of left-wing policies and listened with more patience, if not always with more sympathy.

This failure to communicate persisted throughout the years of Nehru's rule. Sometimes there was a temporary improvement leading to a period of better understanding, but—taking the decade and a half from 1947—there was, for most of the time, an uneasy feeling of constraint between the Indian business community and the prime minister. When Sardar Vallabhai Patel was alive, big business was confident there was someone right at the top who spoke its language and understood its problems; but with Nehru they were never sure. This

gulf between the head of the government and a small but most
important section of the Indian people was the more to be
deplored because some of the best brains in India were to be
found in the ranks of the business sector—as well as some, it
must be said, who had reduced sharp practice in such matters
as tax evasion to a fine art. Unfortunately, Pandit Nehru
lumped them all together and was prone to regard the slick
operators as representative of the whole class. And the public
were only too ready to believe the worst after one or two
notorious company scandals had come to light and the principal
malefactors appeared to go unpunished. Large quantities of
'black' or 'unaccounted' money had escaped the revenue
authorities, and such tax-free fortunes added to inflationary
pressures. Foreign exchange irregularities had become common
form. All the circumstances combined to project Indian private
enterprise on public attention in the worst possible light. Its
critics did not require to look very far for ammunition. The
wiser heads in Indian business saw clearly the need to go some
way towards meeting the prime minister's prejudices, however
ill-conceived they may have thought them to be. In any head-
on clash they knew they were bound to lose. They were also
anxious to prove that they were no less patriotic than any other
Indian.

Yet in spite of his antipathy to private enterprise, which he
took little trouble to disguise, Nehru moved only slowly
towards the final adoption by the Congress Party of the
socialist creed. It was not until the Avadi meeting of the party
in 1955 (to which we have already referred in chapter 2) that
the Congress Party finally passed the resolution on the 'socialist
pattern of society': a formula which is flexible enough to have
some kind of meaning for almost everyone. One may reasonably
ask why, if he felt so strongly, was he content with a diluted form
of socialism such as is expressed in the idea of the socialist
pattern? Some observers have suggested that in the eight years
between 1947 and 1955 Nehru put private enterprise on a
prolonged trial, and that only when he saw that it would not
give India what he wanted in the time he prescribed, did he
turn to socialism. I find this theory unacceptable and I think
that the real truth is that Nehru was a socialist of the heart
rather than the head and that in all economic matters he was

unsure of himself when brought down to details. For this reason he tended to put off major economic decisions until they could no longer be postponed. It would be misleading to give the impression that the Avadi resolution was personal to Nehru; on the contrary it was a full party decision, though he was no doubt glad to have it as a definite mandate.

As things have turned out, India's socialist pattern of society has consisted mainly of the taking into state ownership of a number of commercial and industrial undertakings having special responsibilities towards the community. Detailed mention has been made of them in Chapter 4. In addition the state is expanding its activities through such bodies as the State Trading Corporation, the Metals and Minerals Corporation and the Food Grains Corporation. Between them the institutions acquired or started by government constitute the strategic heights of India's financial and commercial structure, and an administration committed to planning, or to any brand of socialism, was bound to take possession of them. It should be added that in all cases reasonable compensation was paid to the dispossessed private shareholders. This is what one would expect from a government headed by Pandit Nehru, but it is in marked contrast with the conduct of certain other Asian governments, which have compulsorily acquired privately owned foreign or domestic property.

There was nothing very revolutionary in any of these measures, or in such acts as the nationalisation of the airlines and the creation by the state of new sources of power and energy. Does anyone imagine that enough private capital would have been forthcoming to give India three new steel works in less than ten years? If they do, they should read the history of the early struggles of the now giant Tata enterprise. The trouble is that so little of the benefit of these things has yet begun to percolate through society at large and to mitigate the chronic want and poverty which is the uncertain base on which the Indian economy rests.

The evidence suggests that Nehru was a Fabian, in the sense that he believed that socialism had a remedy for most of the ills of mankind. But he was not a Fabian who believed in the inevitability of gradualness, for he was much too impatient of results. Yet it matters little what kind of socialist he really was.

The question is whether his method was the right one for India. Having regard to the many difficulties which that newly independent country has had to overcome (including shortages of technical and managerial manpower, of foreign exchange, of the machines to build other machines), there was probably considerable merit in Nehru's hesitant approach to the somewhat vague goal of a socialist pattern of society. Thus, while it is true to say there was a substantial widening of the field of state-ownership and management during Nehru's years as prime minister, there was not much outward and visible evidence of socialism by the time of his death. The businessmen could go to bed contentedly each night, knowing that his investment would still be there in the morning. The only thing that might disturb his rest was the fear of fresh taxation; for, through the instrumentality of a series of extremely able Finance ministers, Nehru steadily jacked up India's rates of personal and corporate taxation until they are amongst the highest in the world. Against this he gave Indian industries a domestic market that is highly protected by tariffs, import quotas, foreign exchange shortages and other impediments. In effect, he made sure there were some profits to tax.

At the beginning of this chapter, it was stated that Nehru was not an easy man to interview. It might have been added with truth that he was more than usually susceptible to first impressions of a person or proposition. Inevitably, therefore, he made more than one serious misjudgement of men or things. The rapport which he established at his first meeting with Earl Mountbatten in Malaya in the spring of 1946 was definitely not one such, and it was destined to set the pattern for the new and happier chapter of Indo-British relations which was beginning to open up. On the other hand, when he paid his first visit to the United States three years later his mind seems to have received an unfavourable impression from his initial public engagement: a luncheon with a number of bankers and business magnates. It is said that he never quite rid himself of the unfavourable impression that he formed of their total wealth when it was mentioned in the course of a well-meant speech of welcome. He did not give his friendship easily, but once given his loyalty to his friends was firm and strong—and sometimes foolish. At least one cabinet minister, Krishna Menon, was protected by the aura of his friendship long after he had ceased to enjoy the confidence of the people. But this is the sort of thing which is not infrequently a trait of the very great, of whom Nehru was one. Towards the end, with visibly failing health, his hold over the masses was weakening, but it was still immeasurably stronger than that of any other Indian leader.

On a number of occasions he accorded me interviews in connection with my professional work. Of these, three in particular remain prominently in memory. The first was at the home of the late Dr B. C. Roy in Wellington Square, Calcutta in 1942, when the Allied war effort was going about as badly as it could. In a long discussion we talked mostly about the chances of India achieving its freedom as part of the coming peace. Neither of us knew that Ahmednagar Fort was waiting to receive Nehru as a prisoner in a few weeks' time. The second notable meeting was in 1950 at Government House, Calcutta (now Raj Bhavan). He had just signed an agreement with the late Liaquat Ali Khan over treatment of minorities. The air was thick with rumours of armed conflict between India and Pakistan, and rail and river routes from East Pakistan were choked with refugees. Nehru spoke quietly, but with immense sincerity, of the duty laid upon each country to win the trust of its minorities. Four years later, in company with a colleague who knew him well, I saw him soon after he had returned from his visit to China in the autumn of 1954. He was almost lyrical about the economic progress which had been made by the Chinese People's Republic. The subjects discussed on these three occasions represent the themes which dominated the last years of his life: India's freedom; the position of its minorities; the adjustment of its relations with the outside world, particularly Pakistan and China; and finally, the techniques of planning and economic growth.

Nehru lived to see India's freedom fully consummated. Indeed, with Gandhi, he made the major individual contribution to this end. For his share in this his memory will be honoured by Indians everywhere and for all time. The position of India's minorities is likely to remain one of difficulty, if not danger, for as long as we can foresee. Nehru realised that in the end the security of the minority rested upon the restrained and civilised

behaviour of the majority. He felt the partition of his country
keenly, but that he has had some success in the pursuit of a
policy of tolerance may be assumed from the fact that 45 million
Moslems have chosen to remain in India and by natural
processes their number is growing every day. The final pattern
of India's relations with the outside world is still being worked
out, as are its plans for accelerated economic growth. Judged
by the present (winter 1965) state of India's relations with
Pakistan and China, much of Nehru's foreign policy would
seem to have been a failure, and it is clear that his successors
will have to be content with less ambitious and more practical
measures. At the moment of writing, details of the Fourth
Five-Year Plan are still awaited. But the debate about its size
has been going on for some months: is it better to have something attainable or another castle in the air?

The main charge his critics make against him is that Nehru's
policies were invariably too vague and dreamy: his socialism
imprecise; his foreign policy was not sufficiently down-to-earth;
his domestic decrees lacked adequate supporting organisational
effort. There is some truth in all these allegations, but this does
not seriously detract from the greatness of the man. He knew
that the vast amorphous mass which is India could only be
governed and held together by a series of compromises: a concession here, a special exception there. He was the bridge between the generations, the link between the nationalism of the
old freedom movement and the new post-war Asian resurgence.
He guided India through the first difficult years of independence. He secured for his country an honoured place amongst
the nations and gave it a new sense of self-respect. He not only
set India free, but he has also set its course for years to come.

12

POSTSCRIPT

ON MONDAY, November 8, 1965, the Defence minister told
parliament that a total of 2,212 Indian soldiers had been killed
in the Indo-Pakistani clash during August and September;
7,636 were wounded and 1,500 missing. Since the cessation of
the fighting on September 23, 378 Pakistanis and 262 Indians
had been killed in sporadic and relatively minor encounters
along the cease-fire line. By then six weeks of the truce arranged
by the United Nations had elapsed and neither side had withdrawn or disengaged its armies. It remains to be added that,
up to the first week of November, India alleged more than 900
violations of the cease-fire now being supervised by a much
enlarged corps of UN observers. These are some of the chief
statistical dimensions of a war which lasted less than two
months, but whose consequences are likely to prove quite dis-
proportionate to the time-scale on which it was fought.

The origins of the quarrel over Kashmir have been discussed
in chapter 6. Here we can briefly resume that part of the story
which begins in the summer of 1965. The Rann of Kutch affair
has been mentioned on an earlier page; in the light of subsequent
events it cannot be regarded as more than a probing operation
and a curtain-raiser to the sterner events which were to follow.
The satisfaction at the signing in Delhi on June 30 of an agreement to stop the fighting in the Rann was soon dispelled by the
announcement in the Indian capital on August 8 that a large-
scale infiltration into Kashmir was in progress. It was clear,
said the government of India spokesman, that 'the operation
had been planned, organised and equipped in Pakistan', and
this has not been denied—indeed it has been confirmed on the
highest Pakistani authority. The infiltrators, who were stated

to have been under training since early summer, came from Pakistan-held Kashmir and their operations were apparently supported by Pakistani troops firing directly across the 1948 cease-fire line. Whatever view one may take of the genesis of the Kashmir dispute, there can be little doubt that its 1965 resumption was deliberately organised by Pakistan.* Indians feel strongly—and with a good deal of reason—that not sufficient account of this fact has been taken in the West.

Indian sources estimated that between 1,000 and 1,200 Pakistani irregulars were involved in these initial hit-and-run operations along a frontier of about 450 miles. This was the position at the beginning of August, and throughout that month the tempo of the fighting increased. By the time parliament met in New Delhi for its monsoon session, the situation was regarded as extremely grave. The number of 'infiltrators' increased rapidly and by the beginning of September no attempt was made to differentiate between them and Pakistan's regular forces, which had now launched an attack in strength on the Chhamb sector of the Kashmir front. Tanks and aeroplanes were used by both sides for the first time and in a particularly bloody battle Indian forces had to fight desperately to retain control of the Akhnoor bridge, a vital link in the chain of communication with their comrades in Srinagar and other parts of the Vale of Kashmir. The thing which the friends of both countries had always feared had at last happened: India and Pakistan were engaged in a war, the horrors of which were in no way mitigated by the fact that there had never been any formal declaration of hostilities.

In response to a Security Council resolution, both countries agreed to a cease-fire which was formally effective from September 22. In the three weeks of fighting much damage had been done, not merely in a physical sense but in a wider and less tangible way which is not easily identifiable. Two members of the Commonwealth had engaged in deadly combat which it seemed had solved nothing; the conflict had not only created a wide gulf between the two belligerents themselves,

---

* Any doubt on this point will be dispelled by a reading of U Thant's report (5/6651) dated September 3, 1965 to the Security Council, and particularly that part of it which deals with General Nimmo's communications as head of the UN Observer Group in Kashmir.

but between each of them and their traditional friends in the West; both sides had sustained material losses which were sufficiently large to have an effect on their Five Year Plans (India's Fourth Plan due to begin in 1966 and Pakistan's Third which had only run a couple of months when the fighting began); the whole question of a continuance of the international aid on which their economies depend was thrown into hazard; new and unpredictable forces had been unleashed in South Asia. It seemed that the foundations on which Nehru had so carefully built many of his policies had crumbled and collapsed in a few short weeks. Yet by no means all the effects are to be placed on the debit side of the account; most observers agree that India emerged from this short and fierce struggle stronger and more unified than before. Its honour had been redeemed; its armies had succeeded in what had been a war of strictly limited objectives. The defeat by the Chinese of three years earlier (under conditions that were heavily weighted against the Indian forces) had been expunged if not avenged. In a sentence, self-respect was restored.

According to an official spokesman in New Delhi on September 6, India's proclaimed objective was to destroy the bases from which her territory, i.e. Kashmir, was being attacked. By this time India's position in the Chhamb sector had become precarious, and to relieve the pressure on that part of the front Indian forces crossed the West Punjab frontier in a drive towards Lahore, while a second offensive was mounted from the Jammu sector of Kashmir with Sialkot, another important city in Pakistani Punjab, as its target. The purpose was to draw off Pakistani troops that would otherwise be used to strengthen the attack on the Akhnoor bridge. Such a diversion would be a normal military precaution which a commander responsible for the defence of a vital frontier would feel that he was entitled, and perhaps obliged, to take. That apart, in one of his statements at the time of the Rann of Kutch clash, the Indian prime minister had stated that a moment might come when India would have to give battle at a time and place of its own choosing. Such a moment had now arrived.

This development thoroughly alarmed the Security Council and the governments of the West, and within a few hours the British prime minister, Harold Wilson, issued a statement

which was to cause much controversy and to place a heavier
strain on Indo-British relations than anything which has
occurred since independence. The offending words were:

> I am deeply concerned at the increasingly serious fighting
> now taking place between India and Pakistan, and especially
> at the news that Indian forces have today attacked
> Pakistan territory across the international frontier in the
> Punjab. This is a distressing response to the resolution
> adopted by Security Council on September 4, calling for a
> cease fire.
>   The dangerous situation now created may have the
> gravest consequences not only for India but also for the
> peace of the world. . . . No lasting solution of the Kashmir
> problem can possibly be reached by force. . . .

It has to be conceded that, read as it stands (and especially 'at
the news that Indian forces have today attacked Pakistan territory across the international frontier in the Punjab'), the statement must seem to an Indian to do much less than justice to his
country's case. There is no mention of what India regards as
the primary aggression, namely the activities of the original
infiltrators at the beginning of August, and the general presumption of the document is that 'the dangerous situation now
created' was sparked off by the Indian crossing of the Punjab
border. It is highly improbable that Harold Wilson intended to
convey this, but the fact is that in the minds of Indians, who
have never anyway been quite sure of the British attitude over
Kashmir, this was the impression that was left.

Nor was the belief just confined to a few excitable backbench
leftwing politicians or irresponsible journalists. Senior civil
servants and others, who had long been advocates of a close
friendship with Britain, shared these views. The interdict on
the commercial shipment of arms, and the prohibition of the
use of those which had been given as aid against China from
being employed against Pakistan, completed the unhappy, and
largely ineffective, catalogue of intervention which left Indo-
British relations at their lowest ebb for more than twenty years.
They were perhaps the most serious casualty of the war: a condition which is in no way mitigated by the widely and wrongly

held (but skilfully propagated) belief that Britain supported
Pakistan throughout. It is a complete fallacy to think as some
people do that, because Britain was critical of some aspects of
the Indian case over Kashmir, it automatically endorsed
Pakistan's allegations. The fact is that, for the third party, the
tangled web of the Kashmir dispute presents itself as something
in which he sees right and wrong on both sides; as a result he
cannot give to either his full emotional or intellectual support.
Nor can he be one hundred per cent neutral. For those who
have lived and worked in the subcontinent, it presents the sad-
dest and most baffling of the many question marks that the
transfer of power in 1947 has raised.

The end of the fighting on September 23 brought India face
to face with the fact that some of its most sincere friends among
the countries of the world were uneasy about the absolute
confidence with which India had assumed its case over Kashmir
to be absolutely correct. India's military prowess had recently
been demonstrated for all to see; but the consensus of world
opinion seemed to be that, if the Kashmir issue was as straightforward as India claimed, it ought at least to be open to discussion: a proposition which India regarded as a derogation of
its sovereignty. But only one Indian leader lent his powerful
voice to a plain and public statement that India must satisfy
world opinion that the people of Kashmir do really support the
integration of the state into the Indian Union. Writing in
Swarajaya (November 13, 1965) 'Rajaji' (C. Rajagopalachari),
now eighty-six years of age and perhaps the last surviving colleague of Gandhi and Nehru, said:

India's persistent refusal to refer the question to the people
of Kashmir itself raises a presumption in the minds of the
governments of the world that we expect an adverse verdict
if such a reference were made. Although the governance of
Kashmir has been conducted on democratic lines since 1950,
and three elections on the basis of adult suffrage have been
held in that region during this period in which the people of
the Valley and of Jammu and Ladakh have not indicated
that they want a change from accession to India, it is obvious
that the nations of the world and a considerable section of
the people of Kashmir do not feel convinced that these elec-

tions have been uninfluenced by the authority exercised by India in that region.*

But it would be misleading to imply that many Indians would be prepared to go along with 'Rajaji' in this argument. Over the years the strength of public feeling on the Kashmir issue has tended to fluctuate according to the general state of Indo-Pakistani affairs; but generally the trend has been towards increasing rigidity and the taking up of fixed positions. Neither Nehru nor his successor as prime minister, Lal Bahadur Shastri, was able to move far ahead of popular opinion—particularly that part of it which is vociferous in parliament and the press.

Yet in one important respect Nehru's hopes have been amply fulfilled: there were no communal troubles between Hindu and Moslem during the conflict, and by general consent India's 45 million Moslems showed as much patriotism and concern for their country as any other section of the population. Moslem troops fought bravely alongside their Hindu comrades, and in every other way the Moslem community took its due share of the war effort. It is, of course, impossible to say what might have happened had it been a long war in which India sustained a series of heavy defeats. Even so, Nehru's rejection of the two-nation theory, and his concept of the secular state, were fully vindicated at the first major test. The problem of the 10 million Hindus in Pakistan is not quite on the same footing and in any case this is not the place to discuss it, except perhaps to say that if India had the really aggressive intentions that its neighbour claims it would surely have mounted an attack on East Pakistan, where the problems of supplying or reinforcing the defending forces would have been well nigh insuperable.

It may be said that the Chinese and Pakistani conflicts have made nonsense of two main props of Nehru's foreign policy, i.e., non-alignment and *Panch Sila*. Matters of high policy are

* This newspaper article was subsequently the subject of a prosecution by the government of Madras State on the grounds that it was calculated to lead readers to question the territorial integrity of India, prejudice its relations with foreign powers and excite disaffection towards the armed forces. However, Delhi ordered withdrawal of the prosecution.

not to be dismissed in such easy generalisations. Non-alignment undoubtedly made it possible for Russia and India to come closer together in the mid-1950s: a movement which was symbolised by Nehru's visit to Moscow in 1955, which was returned soon after in the form of a three week tour of India by Bulganin and Khrushchev. This was the beginning of an accord between the USSR and India which has given India a certain amount of economic aid as well as diplomatic backing at the United Nations. India has thus acquired a powerful friend without forfeiting the support of the USA, from which by far the largest proportion of the aid for the Five Year Plans has come. It is true that Russia observed a studied neutrality in the 1962 Sino-Indian border clash, but the Kremlin made it quite clear in 1965 that the USSR had no intention of encouraging Chinese intervention in the subcontinent. On that occasion Peking made a major miscalculation, and its attempt to transform the conflict into a passionate anti-American crusade was a complete fiasco.

Indeed the United States of America perhaps holds the key to the future as the major donor of aid. At this stage nothing but informed guesses can be made of the actual financial cost of the military campaign in Kashmir. All that we know for sure is that the figure is almost certainly higher than either side can afford; £50 million for each of the belligerents would probably not be an overestimate for the final bill of costs for the loss of such equipment as planes, tanks and other military hardware, guns and small arms, the destruction of bridges and buildings and railway tracks and the general devastation caused by the fighting. India, which has by now gone a considerable way towards developing a steel-based industrial economy and also possesses a number of efficient ordnance factories, can itself probably make good a much higher proportion of the lost equipment than can Pakistan. But neither country can dodge the issue of the increased taxation needed to replace the depradations of war, and both face the prospect of higher defence budgets for some years to come.

The result must inevitably be to drain off resources that would otherwise have been available for planning purposes; India's dependence on foreign aid and investment for the Fourth Plan will be greater than ever before. A figure of Rs 4,000 crores (£3,000 million) was put before the National Develop-

ment Council at its meeting on September 5, 1965 as being the
gross amount of external assistance that is likely to be necessary
in the period 1966–71. 'Aid Without Strings' can hardly be
made a precondition of assistance on this scale, and it would
not be surprising if India was informed by the USA as the chief
supplier of aid that it will continue to come forward only as long
as there is a reasonable prospect of its being used for peaceful
and productive purposes. Among these latter is the urgent need
for a more forthright agricultural policy to avoid a repetition
of the grave food shortages that are once more looming up
in most of India's cities as this book goes to the press. With
the population growing at a rate of over 2 per cent per annum,
these shortages are even more menacing to the stability of the
subcontinent than they were in the hopeful years of Jawaharlal
Nehru's rule.

Early in January 1966, the leaders of India and Pakistan
accepted a Soviet invitation to meet at Tashkent to settle their
differences under the chairmanship of Alexei Kosygin, head of
the Russian government. Kosygin had first proposed such a
meeting in September 1965, and the initial reactions in
Delhi and Karachi were cautious. The five-day meeting between
Shastri and Ayub Khan was, in all the circumstances, surprisingly successful in that they signed a joint declaration of practical, if limited, scope—though any specific commitment on
the future of Kashmir was avoided. One of its most important
provisions—the withdrawal of the armed forces of both countries to their positions before August 1965—is being implemented as this book goes to press (February 1966), and it is
hoped to make an early start on other matters which the 1965
war has left over for settlement.

The Tashkent conference seems likely to be a triumph for
shrewd Soviet diplomacy. Amongst other things, Russia served
notice on China that it has a continuing interest in South
Asian affairs. It was also a considerable personal achievement
for Kosygin in his country's first major attempt at peace-making
in the region.

But for India, the occasion ended on a tragic note. Shastri,
whose health had always been an uncertain quantity, died of a
sudden heart attack in the early hours of January 11, while

still at Tashkent. His premiership had lasted only eighteen months. The election of his successor, Mrs Indira Gandhi, Nehru's daughter, was quickly and smoothly accomplished. This would have greatly pleased Pandit Nehru, not merely because the new prime minister is his only child, but also because this steady and untroubled leadership-succession reveals an inner strength in the political system which Nehru bequeathed India. It has fairly been said that no nation can be regarded as an effective democracy until it has changed its government by democratic procedure at least once. India has now passed this stern test on two occasions.

REFERENCES

I INTRODUCTORY

1. Joan Robinson, *Economic Philosophy*, Penguin, Harmondsworth and Baltimore, 1964: p. 106.

3 MALTHUSIAN DILEMMA

1. *Second Five Year Plan*, New Delhi, 1956; Chapter IV, 'Finance and Foreign Exchange'.

4 MIDDLE WAY

1. Rafiq Zakaria (ed.), *A Study of Nehru*, published by *Times of India*, Bombay, 1959.
2. H. Vankatasubbia, *India's Economy since Independence*, Asia Publishing House, New Delhi, 1958.
3. Chintaman C. Deshmukh, *Economic Development in India 1946-1956* (Dadabhai Naoraji Memorial Lectures), p. 26.
4. *Ibid.*, p. 14.

6 INDIA AND ITS NEIGHBOURS

1. Ian Stephens, *Pakistan*, Benn, London, 1962; Praeger, New York, 1963: p. 13.
2. Josef Korbel, *Danger in Kashmir*, Princeton University Press, Princeton, 1954; Oxford University Press, London, 1954: p. 25.
3. Report of June 29, 1948 meeting in 'Proceedings of the East India Association', *Asiatic Review*, Vol. XLIV, No. 160, London, October 1948.
4. A reliable summary of the first decade of the imbroglio is given in 'The Kashmir Dispute After Ten Years', *The World Today*, Vol. 14, No. 2, February 1948 (Royal Institute of International Affairs, London).
5. G. E. Harvey, *British Rule in Burma 1824-1942*, Faber, London, 1946.

7 CHINA AND BORDER STATES

1. *The Times*, January 13, 1965.
2. Alastair Lamb, *The China-India Border: the Origins of the Disputed Boundaries*, Oxford University Press, London and New York, for the Royal Institute of International Affairs, 1964.
3. Sir Francis Tuker, *Gorka: The Story of the Gurkhas of Nepal*, Constable, London, 1957; Author's Foreword.
4. Regarding American financial support, see Eugene B. Mihaly, 'Developments in Nepal', *The World Today*, Vol. 19, No. 10, October 1963 (Royal Institute of International Affairs, London).

8 THE COMMONWEALTH

1. Devaluation Debate, Constituent Assembly, October 5 and 6, 1949.
2. Anthony Eden (Lord Avon), *Full Circle*, Cassell, London, 1960; Houghton Mifflin, Boston, 1960.
3. *The Hindu*, Madras, August 20, 1956.
4. Quoted in James Eayrs, *The Commonwealth and Suez: A Documentary Survey*, Oxford University Press, London and New York, 1964: p. 8
5. *Ibid.*, p. 86.
6. *Ibid.*, p. 397.
7. See S. R. Mehrota, 'Gandhi and the British Commonwealth', *India Quarterly*, Vol. XVII, No. 2, January-March 1961, p. 49.

9 THE LANGUAGE QUESTION

1. The only report of Lal Bahadur Shastri's statement available to the author has been the summary contained in the official *India News*, February 6, 1965, issued by India House, London.
2. V. P. Menon, *The Integration of the Indian States*, Longmans, London, 1956; Macmillan, New York, 1956.
3. *Report of the States Reorganisation Commission*, New Delhi, 1955: p. 229.
4. Sir Percival Griffiths, *Modern India*, 3rd edn, Benn, London, 1962; Praeger, New York, 1962.
5. Jawaharlal Nehru, *The Discovery of India*, Signet Press, Calcutta, 1946; John Day, New York, 1946: p. 295.

10 PARTY LEADER AND HEAD OF ADMINISTRATION

1. W. H. Morris-Jones, *The Government and Politics of India*, Hutchinson, London, 1964: p. 200.
2. H. V. R. Iengar, 'Sardar's Ways', Indian Express, May 31, 1965.

11 A TRIAL BALANCE

1. Sir Arthur Lewis, 'Beyond African Dictatorship: The Crisis of the One-Party State', *Encounter*, No. 143, London, August 1965.
2. Kurt Mendelssohn, 'Science in India', *Listener*, London, September 24, 1964.
3. Rafiq Zakaria, *op. cit.*, p. 18.

INDEX

202 INDEX

China—*cont.*
relations with Russia, 63, 75;
supported by India at UN, 76, 102;
see also Tibet
Chittagong, 117
Chota Nagpur, 180
Chou En-lai, 71, 73–4, 112–13; visits
Delhi, 104, 107
Churchill, Sir Winston, 3
Civil disobedience, 4, 170
Civil Service, 6, 8, 68, 168–71
Colombo, 96, 113; Plan, 43 n., 120
Commonwealth affairs, 71–2, 123–37;
Prime Ministers' Conferences, 5,
123–4, 128
Communist Party, Indian, 63, 150,
159–60
Congress Party, 69, 74, 158–67, 170,
173; advocates break with Common-
wealth, 123; Nehru's presidency of,
4–5, 7, 15, 19, 69, 157 ff.; on lan-
guage problems, 147; resignation of
ministers, 162; socialist policies of,
25, 51, 184
Councils, advisory, 63–4
Cripps, Sir Stafford, 126
Czechoslovakia, 57

Dalai Lama, 103, 105, 110, 119
De Gaulle, Charles, 3
Delhi, New Delhi: Chou En-lai in,
104, 107, conferences at, 49, 72–3,
86, 122, 128, 143, 145–6, 161; gossip
in, 158–9; government, 11, 68–9, 82,
84, 93, 97, 109–10, 150, 164–6, 189–
91; Nehru's speeches in, 67, 99; Suez
crisis reactions, 134; University of, 53
Desai, Morarji, 160, 162–4, 166–7
Deshmukh, Shri C. D., 59, 165
Digboi oilfields, 109
Discovery of India, The, 4, 152, 156
Dorji, Jigme, 119–20
Dravida Munnetra Kazagham, 152,
161
Dulles, John Foster, 128, 131–2
Durgapur steelworks, 45

East India Association, 81
East India Company, 55, 93, 119
Eayrs, James, 135
Eden, Sir Anthony (Earl of Avon),
129, 131–2, 135
Edward VIII, 169

Egypt, 113, 128–35, 178
Eisenhower, Dwight D., 3, 75
'Employment opportunities', 37–8
Ethiopia, 131
Export-Import Council, 64

Farming: collective, 57–8; co-opera-
tive, 58; *see also* Agriculture
Farrukhsiar, Emperor, 3
Fiji, 60
Five Principles of Peaceful Co-Exist-
ence: *see* Panch Shila
Five Year Plans, 6, 11–12, 22–50, 54,
56, 174, 195; First, effects of, 34–8;
Second, aims of, 39–41; results, 44;
Third, 44–50; Fourth, 65–6, 188, 191
195; Pakistan's, 191
Food production: *see* Agriculture
Formosa: *see* Taiwan
France, French, 43, 93, 129; in Suez
crisis, 132–6
Franks, Lord, 45–7
Freedom Movement, 53; *see also*
Swatantra

Galbraith, John K., 64 n.
Gandhi, Mrs Indira, 85, 158–9, 197
Gandhi, Mahatma, 6–8, 15–17, 19, 51,
62, 148 n., 163; attitude to caste, 153;
attitude to Commonwealth, 137;
influence on Nehru, 4, 16–17, 112,
187
Gangtok, 120
Ghana, 113
Ghosh, Atulya, 166
Gilgit, 83
Goa, 7, 93–4
Goalpara, 149
Government of India Act, 11
Grierson, Sir G., 139–40
Gujerat, 56, 150, 164, 177
Gulab Singh, Maharajah, 81
Gurkhas, 114

Harijan, 153
Harrow School, 4, 16
Harvey, G. E., 97
Himalayan states, 100–22
Hindi: *see* Language
Hitler, Adolf, 132
Hongkong, 60
Hungary, rising in, 134
Hyderabad, 68, 94, 134, 147, 149–50

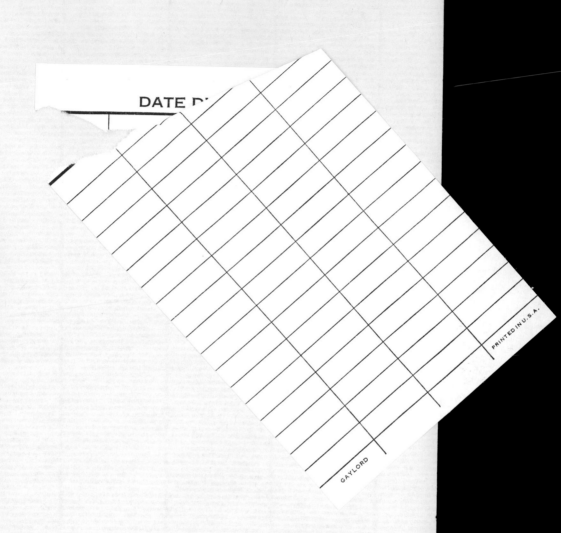

GAYLORD

PRINTED IN U.S.A.